JEFF IMMELT

- AND THE NEW -

GE WAY

INNOVATION, TRANSFORMATION, AND WINNING IN THE 21ST CENTURY

DAVID MAGEE

New York   Chicago   San Francisco   Lisbon
London   Madrid   Mexico City   Milan   New Delhi
San Juan   Seoul   Singapore   Sydney   Toronto

1 2 3 4 5 6 7 8 9 0   DOC/DOC   0 1 0 9

ISBN: 978–0–07–160587–8
MHID: 0–07–160587–8

This publication is designed to provide accurate and authoritative information in regard to the subject matter covered. It is sold with the understanding that the publisher is not engaged in rendering legal, accounting, or other professional service. If legal advice or other expert assistance is required, the services of a competent professional person should be sought.

—From a Declaration of Principles Jointly Adopted by a Committee of the American Bar Association and a Committee of Publishers and Associations

McGraw-Hill books are available at special quantity discounts to use as premiums and sales promotions, or for use in corporate training programs. To contact a representative, please visit the Contact Us pages at www.mhprofessional.com.

This book is printed on acid-free paper.

CONTENTS

CONTENTS

INTRODUCTION

Perhaps no company in the world and its management have been studied over recent decades as closely as General Electric, the long-successful, multidimensional corporation known for its prowess and innovation, respect and reliability. Say, "GE" to almost any student of business, and expect in return a well-versed response of insight and opinion considering that for over a century the company has been one of the world's biggest and best. As one of the original 12 companies comprising the Dow Jones Industrial Average (1896), General Electric morphed decades ago into a conglomerate and diversified from its original incarnation as an electrical company. It was founded by Thomas Edison, who pioneered the incandescent electric lamp.

Through merger, acquisition, and strategic growth, GE became one of the largest companies in the world in terms of market capitalization (more than $300 billion), annual sales and profits ($172 billion and $22 billion in 2007), and admiration (ranked first in the world by *Fortune* magazine in 2007), participating in an array of industries including technology, media, and finance.

With more than 300,000 worldwide employees and business diversification which creates everything from jet engines and home appliances to television shows, GE files America's most detailed annual tax return (more than 20,000 pages) and has long been a worthy and necessary benchmark of business study. Likely no corporation or its corporate leadership has been examined like that of General Electric, ranging from numerous top-selling commercial books (including *Jack Welch and the GE Way* by Robert Slater and *Control Your Own Destiny or Someone Else Will* by Noel Tichy) to literally dozens of in-depth academic studies.

Based in Fairfield, Connecticut, the multinational corporation was legendary long before a leader named John Francis "Jack" Welch Jr. took control of the company as chairman and CEO in 1981, but it was under his 20-year tenure that the "GE way" became a lexicon of leadership for almost anyone interested in enterprise excellence.

If you said "Jack" on Wall Street in the 1980s and 1990s, most people knew immediately who you were talking about; if you said "Jack" around any of General Electric's global employees during the same time frame you could expect those in earshot to look over a shoulder to see whether their effervescent boss was around before articulating appropriately. Welch commanded that kind of attention. He was an icon running an icon, a kind of brand within a brand, during a robust business growth environment when talented and ambitious leaders and the companies they ran could seemingly do no wrong. When Welch talked, his zest and pragmatism defined what was becoming of the hard-charging era:

Get better or get beaten!
Get the most out of your employees.
Stop managing, start leading.

Lessons learned from such recitation and study were invaluable. When Jack Welch and GE pared costs during unprecedented periods of growth, shareholders were consistently rewarded with strong earnings and stock price growth. No big company in the world had ever achieved such significant and lasting results, with revenues increasing more than fourfold, and share price increasing more than 20-fold in two decades. Study shows that leadership successfully collided with America's economic boom period in the latter half of the twentieth century to effectively produce both growth and yield.

Yet times change, and so does the business environment. The world quickly became a different place from almost the moment Jack Welch left not long after the dawning of the twenty-first century, turning over his job as GE chairman and CEO to long-time company employee Jeffrey Immelt. Not only did Immelt inherit a large, quite mature company at the end of a remarkable two-decade run, but he took office in 2001 just four days before the 9/11 terrorist attacks on the United States, the first of several events which set the world on a decidedly more sobering and difficult path than it experienced in the go-go 1990s. The economy slowed. The stock market bubble deflated. The housing bubble deflated. Credit markets suffered. Corporations became more impact-accountable. Gas prices rose. Consumer confidence and buying power waned.

The house that Jack built was not nearly on so firm a foundation. And yet during Immelt's first seven years on the job General Electric's revenue increased by 60 percent and profits doubled, causing Pulitzer Prize–winning journalist Steven Pearlstein of *The Washington Post* to proclaim in 2008, "Jeff Immelt is probably one of the best corporate executives on the planet."

The point, of course, is not to spread effusive praise by using the remark. Anyone even loosely tracking Immelt during his leadership tenure understands that criticisms of him have been all over the map because of the troubled environment that so abruptly emerged after the turn of the century.

But the point should not be missed: Leading an enormously large, mature company to growth and a reshaped, promising future in a most difficult environment is worthy of study in its own right; more so perhaps than study of high-yield harvest in bountiful years when growing conditions aligned perfectly. The championship football coach who once said his best season was leading a rebuilding team to a 7–3 record can relate. So can the sales manager who coaxed growth from a well-sold product line while her predecessor benefitted from launch.

Simply, arrival of the twenty-first century signaled the dawning of a new economy, one with new lessons to be learned; one where winning is defined not only by immediate results but also by how a corporation contributes to long-term sustainability of both its operations and its endeavors and the world at large. That is why when Immelt assumed the leadership position of one of the world's largest and consistently best corporations, he adopted one of his predecessor's key business philosophies, before quickly evolving one of his own:

Embrace change, don't fear it.

In more than seven years on the job, Immelt managed challenging circumstances and a changing view of the future with his specialized leadership style. Just like his predecessors, he made mistakes, of course. He faced heavy criticism in 2008, including harsh words from Welch, his former boss, by failing to recognize a single quarterly earnings miss before it was made public, and he admittedly did not expect financing businesses to face the exposure they did. Shareholders often debate whether his vision is too long term for short-term returns; as a result, analysts constantly debate his assimilation of the conglomerate's puzzle.

In the hardest of times, however, Immelt's leadership is undeniably reshaping GE into a different and more contemporary corporation; one he believes will be able to profit and move more nimbly forward in the new global economy. Demands of the twenty-first century are much different from those faced by Immelt's predecessor, Welch, and in accordance, strategies and styles have changed. This is the story of what Jeff Immelt is doing at GE and why—and what we can learn from it.

CHAPTER 1

FOLLOWING A LEADER

"Leadership is about confidence and I always knew
I could do this job."

—JEFF IMMELT

Jeff Immelt jokes that he had one really good day on the job after taking over as chairman and CEO of General Electric in 2001 before trouble struck. He knew that replacing Jack Welch, who grew the company exponentially during America's robust economic growth period at the end of the twentieth century while becoming a true celebrity CEO, would not be easy. The last thing he wanted to do was go down in history as another Phil Bengston.

A former University of Minnesota All-American tackle who became an assistant football coach right after graduating from college in 1934, Bengston made several stops in the NCAA and NFL before joining Vince Lombardi's Green Bay Packers staff. He was the only coach to last the full nine seasons with Lombardi. Serving as defensive coordinator, his low-key approach blended well with the fiery Lombardi, and the Packers won five NFL titles and the first two Super Bowls under their leadership.

When Lombardi left in 1967, Bengston was hired as head coach, but he was let go after three seasons with a losing record.

Most observers believe that Bengston never had a chance as the Packer's head coach. Green Bay's star players were aging. The Packers had already been to the pinnacle several times. Fans were so used to Lombardi and his ruthless, winning ways that no replacement would be good enough. After all, there was only one Vince Lombardi.

Like the legendary Packers coach, known to be at times aloof and angry with players, Jack Welch was not perfect as a corporate leader despite a titanic reputation. He failed in attempts to make money with retailer Montgomery Ward and brokerage firm Kidder Peabody. He was not able to pull off a $45 billion bid for technology and manufacturing company Honeywell at the end of his reign. And some of Welch's famed strategies, including continual cost-cutting and a focus on the American consumer showed flaws near the end of his managerial run.

Still, like Lombardi, Welch went out on top as an unrivaled winner, and history shows that there was only one Jack Welch in twentieth-century U.S. business. So following in his footsteps would not be easy for anyone, regardless of preparation or pedigree.

Immelt approached the job with all the self-confidence a person would need to follow in the footsteps of a legendary leader and run one of the most diversified, successful, and respected companies in the world. Drawing upon an Ivy League education (Dartmouth undergraduate; Harvard MBA) and more than 25 years of shouldering many heavy responsibilities as a GE employee, he knew in the deepest reaches of his mind that he could ably lead the conglomerate well into the twenty-first century.

The Competitor

Born in Cincinnati, Ohio, in 1956, Jeffrey R. Immelt is the son of a school teacher and a retired GE employee who put in 38 years of service. From an early age, his parents—Joseph, who was a middle manager in the GE Aircraft Division, and Donna, who taught elementary school—emphasized the value of learning for Jeff and his older brother, Steve.

"(My parents) believed that a good education was the great social equalizer, something that stays with you your whole life and that allows anyone to live their dreams," said Immelt.

While attending Finneytown High School, Immelt was known as a fierce competitor, buffering his battle to be the best with a comfortable personal style. As a prep basketball player, for instance, he once spoke up to the coach in front of the team, suggesting that the coach was yelling at the players too much. Immelt remembers catching the coach off guard with his bold assessment. But then, he said, the coach took his advice, backing off from his verbal lashings to the team.

Immelt was an A student in high school, and sports were a passion. He liked the measurements provided in the classroom and on the playing field, places where grades and scores yielded tangible, quantifiable results. Standing six-feet four inches tall with a firm handshake and full, bushy hair, Immelt was an imposing presence on the football field. An offensive lineman, he wanted to play in college at an Ivy League school. Dartmouth provided the very complementary academic/athletic collegiate opportunity he was looking for.

"Sports or other competitive collaborative activities are an exceptional way to develop leadership, teamwork, and the ability to deal with success and failure," says Immelt.

According to classmates at Darmouth, Immelt was a beloved, all-around student, getting As in the classroom as he did in high school, playing football, and having so many friends it could at times be burdensome. A member of the Phi Delta Alpha fraternity freshman pledge class of 1974 with Immelt, Jeff Crowe recalls being struck immediately by the "very, very quick-witted, natural born leader." Immelt pledged Phi Delta Alpha, reputed as a more "social" and "beer drinking" fraternity, even though more Dartmouth football players were members of another. From day one, says Crowe, "it was a foregone conclusion that Jeff would be president of the fraternity."

Immelt was, of course, named to the fraternity leadership position as a junior. The Wednesday chapter meetings could be raucous affairs, with one brother trying to outshine another. Yet Immelt possessed a take-charge ability, his classmate says.

He was a leader on the football team as well. In the huddle, Immelt was calm in the heat of battle, typically making jokes talking with teammates about subjects other than the play at hand to diffuse pressure. He might make light-hearted fun of an opposing defender or remind the quarterback of a bonehead move the weekend before.

Immelt was named captain of the football team his senior year, and he held similar status with his fellow math major students. He was popular throughout campus, friends with virtually the entire Dartmouth student body. He liked to have a few beers and laughs with friends, but he was also serious with a keen eye on the value of education.

"Jeff was in high demand," recalls Crowe, today a partner in a venture capital firm in Palo Alto, California. "Somebody was always looking for him to do something, to hang out. But Jeff was determined. He would sneak out of his room at the fraternity house and go down the fire escape and go to the Catholic Student Center so he could study by himself.

"That is still a standing joke about Jeff among his fraternity brothers."

In the summertime in college, Immelt returned home to Cincinnati and worked at a Ford Motor Company assembly plant, taking cues from employees on how they responded to interaction with management. At graduation, Immelt was given an award for character voted on by the entire senior class—he once passed the high honor off in a show of humility by suggesting in a joke that it was given to the student who could chug the most beer—and five years later at the first class reunion he was selected by peers to address the class.

"That shows you what people thought of Jeff," Crowe says. "This was an Ivy League school with a lot of talented people who could easily fill that role."

Immelt remembers the year he graduated from Dartmouth—1978—was a tumultuous time in the world, filled with uncertainty.

"High oil prices had pushed the economy into recession," he said. "Jobs were hard to find, and unemployment was over 10 percent. There was unrest in the Middle East. Americans were being held hostage in Iran."

With a Bachelor of Science degree in applied mathematics, he took a job with Procter & Gamble, briefly sharing an office with future Microsoft CEO Steve Ballmer, himself a new company hire. But Immelt did not stay at Procter & Gamble long, enrolling one year later in Harvard's MBA program. In Boston, he lived with friends from Dartmouth, who noted upon Immelt's taking a job with GE in 1982 that if he stayed at the company for the duration of his career, he would likely end up as CEO. And apparently, his friends were not the only ones noticing Immelt's confidence and poise.

When Immelt was interviewed for the GE job while at Harvard, he met with eventual company vice chairman Dennis Dammerman, who was so struck by the young prospect's poise that he sent his application "straight to managers" so the application would not "get lost in the mix." Immelt was hired in the company's commercial leadership track training which meant that he would work in jobs across GE's diversified businesses before landing a management position.

"He was the best guy I saw that day," recalled Dammerman, who would become one of several key mentors to Immelt during his GE career.

Following in his father's footsteps as a GE employee, Immelt started as an internal sales consultant in the marketing department at company headquarters in Fairfield, Connecticut. From the start, he was not just another employee, having been marked by Dammerman as one to watch, making the company's list of 5,000 employees worth watching and evaluating for management advancement. Within one year of his being hired, Immelt was moving along the upward track, promoted to the company's plastics division based in Dallas, Texas, as a district sales manager.

Immelt's timing in joining GE could not have been better considering all business barometers were pointing upward for the company and a new, aggressive CEO named Welch was barely into his second year leading the company. Welch himself followed a well-respected business leader, succeeding Reginald H. Jones in 1981 after Welch was chosen from a pool of qualified candidates in a succession contest. Welch wasted no time in restructuring the company Jones built, eliminating more than 100,000 jobs in his first few years in office and literally writing and delivering in the early 1980s the preamble to how to grow a business in a slow-growth economy.

Welch's road map to success was no secret to those who studied his style:

- Sell old-line businesses.
- Acquire number one or two businesses in segment or businesses which strengthen GE's number one or two businesses in segment.
- Cut costs and jobs.
- Eliminate bureaucracy.
- Cultivate bottom-up employee initiative.
- Push management hard from the top down to outperform expectations.

Lessons Learned

In the beginning of Welch's tenure, many GE employees cringed at the rapid-fire, shrink-to-grow management strategy he employed. The company was profitable and respected when

Welch took over, yet he was cutting jobs by the thousands! In response, some in the media and inside the company nicknamed him Neutron Jack, presenting him as a corporate villain.

Jeff Immelt was not among Welch's critics. Welch could be excruciatingly demanding, but from the moment he took over until he retired in 2001, says Immelt, Welch was the right leader at the right time. Like Dammerman, Welch soon became a mentor for the up-and-coming company manager. Immelt, in fact, got to make a presentation before Welch in 1982, just 30 days after going to work for GE in marketing. The meeting was in contrast to a prediction by a Morgan Stanley partner trying to woo Immelt to work for the financial company. Immelt was told if he went to work for GE, he would likely not even meet Welch for another decade. In just one month, however, he was in a meeting with Welch.

Dating back to its founding in the late 1800s, GE's culture was based on a hire-the-best, train-them-well, and promote-from-within process built on the premise of creating strengths for the future from the already-existing foundation, thus resulting in long-term sustainability. When Welch took over in 1981, for example, the company had results-oriented management practices in place but needed to be leaner and more aggressive in acquisition to grow. So Welch went to work. History shows he was more of a trailblazer than a status quo executive, but many observers and employees did not really understand either the methods or the madness of his actions at first.

Shrink the workforce to grow the company?

This corporate concept was foreign at the time.

Soon enough, however, GE's stock price was ticking higher and higher, soaring over the span of two decades from a market capitalization of $14 billion to more than $400 billion. Revenues were growing fast as well, and it was not long before U.S. CEOs were mimicking Welch's harsh-talking, results-oriented style.

Throughout his career, Welch could be a hard man to work for if you did not like direct, confrontational criticism. But if you made or exceeded your numbers as a manager, he was quick to reward with generous bonuses and stock options, as Immelt found out in his first big assignment as regional sales manager for GE Plastics in Dallas, where he oversaw 15 direct reports. He got off to a robust start and had a good feeling about Welch and the future of GE.

Immelt knew from his nearly four decades with GE of the company's reliability, but he also sensed that GE's best days were ahead. Immelt was willing to do the work necessary to get the job done, sending the company and his career to a loftier perch. He was a Harvard MBA, but he was not above finding solutions even if it meant working the manufacturing floor.

"I was in El Paso on a Friday visiting a customer, and our product wouldn't work," recalls Immelt. "The customer was irate! So I called our factory. They told me that we couldn't get a replacement product until Monday. I spent the entire weekend fixing and packaging parts with my customer. It never crossed my mind to say to them … 'I can't do this; I have a college degree!'"

From overseeing his first group of direct reports, Immelt says he learned to manage everything from "crusty veterans" to "young hotshots." He also learned in pushing for sales growth at the plastics division during tough economic conditions that GE was all about monthly and quarterly results, or else.

"My manager called and said, 'You had a terrible month. I don't care if you have an MBA from Harvard, I'm not keeping you if you have another bad month.' He was just that direct," said Immelt. "So I learned that in GE you've got to get results. I also learned how to sell and how to manage people who were different from me. I really learned a lot from that experience."

In his early years, among the most valuable lessons learned by Immelt was humility. For instance, during a meeting with Larry Bossidy, the retired CEO of Allied Signal (now Honeywell) and best-selling business book author who spent 30 years rising through the ranks of GE, Immelt proudly bragged on his yearly sales results, which increased by 30 percent from the year before and were just 2 percent over his stretch forecast.

GE's executive in charge of plastics, Bossidy responded bluntly, "To what do you attribute your poor forecasting?"

CHAPTER 2

CONFIDENTLY SEIZE OPPORTUNITY

"Generationally, you know, there are a lot of different styles that are out there. What you've got to do is have a style that works for you, and you have to have a style that works in the time that you're in."

—JEFF IMMELT

B ecause Jeff Immelt was pegged from his first day working at GE as one to watch and cultivate for executive opportunity, he was on the fast track to responsibility. Jack Welch was personally involved in GE's assessment of its top managers, and by the mid-1980s, Immelt's marks, based on criteria including results and the integrity upon which those results were achieved, were consistently high. GE Plastics was a solid proving ground for Immelt a good fit in many respects considering he was natural in the sales role, able to motivate employees and invigorate customers. GE Plastics is also where Immelt met his future wife, division employee Andrea Allen, a customer service representative.

Andrea moved to Chicago on a GE job transfer not long after they met, but she and Immelt kept dating despite the distance;

they married in 1986. A year later they had a daughter, Sarah. Soon afterward, Immelt's career would vault from that of a young and promising MBA hire to a high-potential executive candidate. By 1987 Immelt was among 150 young, high-potential managers being closely watched by Welch and the human resources team for advanced company leadership opportunities. Under an appointment approved by Welch, Immelt also attended that year the executive development course (EDC) at GE's leadership training center at Crotonville, New York. Immelt was the youngest of anyone there.

"Beyond the knowledge you gain (at EDC)," Immelt said, "the best part is just absorbing the culture and the values. And the networking makes you feel that you're part of something great."

Immelt assumed that a bigger job assignment was coming relatively soon after the leadership training, expecting it to be in a GE division outside of plastics. In 1989 he got an unexpected call, however. Jack Peiffer, GE's senior vice president for human resources, told Immelt that he was being offered a job in the company's consumer appliance division in Louisville, Kentucky.

At first, Immelt thought the offer might not be a promotion at all. In the 1980s, plastics were big, and few markets were bigger and more exciting than the plastics market in Dallas in the midst of its heyday. Immelt was an Ivy League man working for one of the world's most respected companies. He was earning good pay in an emerging city with a distinct touch of flair. Louisville, for the moment, was hardly in its heyday, a part-Midwestern, part-Southern river city that boomed in the early twentieth century on manufacturing but was struggling and in need of reinvention in the latter part of the twentieth century.

Initially, Immelt was not terribly excited about going to Louisville, even as the head of customer service for GE Appliances—the number two producer of consumer appliances in the United States behind Whirlpool. The division was in the midst of a massive product recall, and Immelt knew nothing about appliances. His assignment involved compressors for consumer refrigerators, and GE faced massive recalls resulting from faulty manufacturing. With one of the biggest appliance divisions in the United States, a recall for compressors in consumer refrigerators resulted in a significant challenge. He would have to oversee some 7,000 employees scattered across multiple disciplines when previously he had managed only several hundred in mostly sales and marketing functions.

"You've got to be kidding me," said Immelt, when told he was expected to move from plastics in Dallas to consumer appliances in Louisville. "It was like being sent to the far side of the moon."

Immelt was told that Welch wanted someone from outside of appliances to handle the recall situation, so he made the move to Louisville, understanding that the invitation was not one he could turn down if he wanted to continue rising in the ranks at GE.

The assignment was a test. Welch had given Immelt the challenge to see if he could fix the ailing business and survive professionally. Immelt immersed himself in the job, seizing opportunity and turning it into a career-vaulting experience.

Hands-on Experience

In moving to Kentucky, Immelt went from the easier corporate life—running a high-profit, sales-oriented business with a couple of hundred employees—to having 7,000 union-member manufacturing employees to worry about in consumer service. Not to mention, he says, the refrigerator compressors division was in the middle of the biggest crisis that the business had ever experienced. Morale was low in the employee-dense division, and GE's reputation was at stake.

Compressors were failing and needed to be fixed. The balance sheet would take a hit. No question about it. No Harvard case study or his years on the job in Dallas prepared Immelt for what he faced.

A good day at the office became survival.

Immelt wore stress from the job physically. He picked up bad eating habits, snacking at his desk to feed nervous energy. The long hours, lack of activity outside of the office, and poor diet added more than 60 pounds to his once-lean frame (he later lost the weight and has kept it off with regular morning exercise). Immelt's physical transformation on the job was so obvious to all that when he left GE Appliances, employees gave Immelt as a going away gift a cartoon drawing showing him stressed at his desk, surrounded by junk food.

"It was hard," says Immelt. "I was 33 years old and had never had that kind of experience. Before, I was in sales and marketing. All at once I had to learn how to manage people and problems in a distributed network."

For Immelt, though, the chance to captain the unfamiliar ship that was taking on water was the ultimate apprenticeship for leadership. He could no longer rely merely on the sales skills he used in Dallas at GE Plastics. Now Immelt was intricately involved in the business operations at GE Appliances, analyzing financial and quality improvements.

He learned how to work with and motivate union employees, communicating the dire situation while stirring in messages of hope. He learned that direct honesty and clarity in such situations were more effective than hopeful spin. He gave motivational speeches to union workers from atop a forklift on the factory floor. And, he learned that he did not know much about repairing compressors, though he was not afraid to try.

Wearing an appliance repairman's uniform, Immelt rode with technicians fixing faulty GE refrigerator compressors in the field, often participating hands-on in the repair job.

"I remember crawling down on the floor, reaching my hand under the unit, with melting ice cream running down my arm," he says 20 years later, leaning back in a chair in his Fairfield office, smiling to suggest the bad memory has become a good one over time. "I was the worst screwdriver guy in the history of the company, but I did it."

When Immelt met with Welch to talk about performance of the appliance division, discussions were not easy. Welch was closely involved in the situation since the ailing division was a company laggard, dragging down profits with the costly recalls. Immelt figured honesty rather than false optimism should be his best device. Thus he gave Welch only the bare facts, bad as they were.

"I didn't have one good thing to say," Immelt recalled. "I never said, 'Wow, things are great.' Instead, I said, 'We fixed another million compressors this year. Here's how much it cost.' The business lost money for two years. Every line was going straight down. You learned how to motivate people during a tough time, and you learned how to keep your own wits and not to panic. If you panic, everybody goes with you pretty fast."

Immelt was forced to deliver his management results face to face to Welch, the man who was already a business legend in the making. Known for using loudness and profanity while dressing down managers who did not make numbers, Welch heard so much bad news from Immelt that he almost did not believe the reports and was uncharacteristically awkward in response. Immelt's delivery was not a case of a manager gritting his teeth, delivering bad news first; this was bad news first, in the middle, and at the end. Immelt had inherited a business challenge of the highest level.

"I'd say, 'Here's the Weibel curve, Jack, it's going like this,'" said Immelt. "And he would say, 'No, it isn't. You can't be right. You can't possibly be right.' And I would tell him, 'Well, actually, Jack, I am right, and it's going to cost us a couple of hundred million bucks.' And he would say, 'That can't possibly be true.' And I would say, 'Well, it actually is true.' That was a great experience. Thank God I got it. Only a guy like Jack would have had enough faith in a guy like me. Seeing that has made me understand the need to take chances on people."

Welch observed as Immelt calmly handled what might have seemed for some managers like an unwinnable situation. Immelt learned survival skills and an ability to cope and adapt using his own devices. In sales at GE Plastics, he learned how to grow a business. Here, he faced problem solving and acute management. And, while the situation seemed grim, with the division losing money for two years, Immelt turned both the business model and morale in an entirely different direction.

Not too long after he arrived, profits were restored and the factory returned to quality production. In the end, Immelt says, the period was one in which he went "from being a boy to a man." He felt victorious the way a soldier might feel at the end of boot camp. No job could have trained him like the humbling experience in Kentucky.

GE's leadership and Welch in particular took notice. The company was already one of the best at grooming skilled managers for leadership positions, and Immelt's success in passing the stringent test with exemplary grades earmarked him for more upward opportunity within the company.

"Surviving is part of the challenge," Immelt says. "A lot of leadership is based on confidence, and I came away from that experience believing I could overcome almost any workplace challenge."

As reward for his management performance in Louisville, Immelt was sent back to his old division in Dallas, this time as vice president and general manager of GE Plastics, overseeing 5,000 employees and $3 billion in business.

The job started out promising enough. Seeking ways to grow the business, Immelt persuaded primarily U.S. automakers to use more plastic parts. The strategy worked well at first, with division orders soaring. The successful start was impressive enough to earn him a spot on GE's list of 24 company leaders being considered to replace Welch upon his retirement which was planned for sometime around the turn of the century.

But in the mid-1990s the global plastics market fell into a quick inflationary burst, with prices rising for new and recycled goods. Immelt says that he did not react quickly enough to increase pricing to keep pace with the division's rise in cost of goods, and he paid a price. Briefly, the expanded exposure on contracts from the new automotive business took a heavy toll on sales and profits as his division delivered in 1994 a profit growth of only 7 percent against a goal of 20 percent. Revenues were off by $50 million. And Jeff Immelt, GE's rising star executive, fell momentarily under Jack Welch's ever-watchful eye.

At the company's annual meeting of top executives in Boca Raton, Florida, in early 1995, Immelt tried to avoid Welch for three days, knowing what the boss had in store. This is the annual meeting for which Welch was famous; gathering his top people for drill-sergeant type inspiration and lashing as a human resources tool. Miss your numbers, for whatever reason, and pay the price with the company's commander-in-chief. A couple of hundred of GE's top managers were in an auditorium for the meeting. Welch was leading the show. Immediately afterward, Immelt tried to slip out quickly.

Welch grabbed him from behind.

"Jeff," Welch told Immelt, "I'm your biggest fan, but you just had the worst year in the company. Just the worst year. I love you, and I know you can do better. But I'm going to take you out if you can't get it fixed."

Welch knew Immelt was caught in a difficult squeeze play, suffering under quick-shifting and uncontrollable economic conditions, but he had pushed him to get the problem fixed regardless because of the impact on the company's cherished bottom line. Immelt had already taken care of the situation before the boss' admonishment, and he did it by showing a tougher side that many had not seen before.

In a meeting in Detroit with a senior General Motors executive, Immelt had pleaded for a pricing increase, explaining how detrimental the situation would be to both companies if the automaker did not cooperate. The executive said no, and Immelt became agitated. This was Immelt's biggest customer. If he lost General Motors—at the time the largest automaker in the world—there was no replacement.

Immelt's instinct as a salesman was to give the customer the benefit of the doubt. But this was sink or swim. Immelt and the GM executive almost came to physical blows at the meeting, and afterward Immelt was on the phone with General Motors chairman and CEO Roger Smith. In the end, Immelt got a break by effectively presenting GM with analysis that showed how its productivity could be improved by negotiating a compromise. Eventually GM relented, and Immelt had scored another success.

Yet even though the breakthrough came before Welch's official dressing down, Immelt accepted the harsh criticism, understanding that it was obligatory; part of Jack's way and GE's results-oriented culture where consequences typically met numbers misses. Immelt knew that he was not really about to lose his job since the problem was fixed, but he also knew that excuses were not in order.

"Look," Immelt replied to the castigating Welch. "If the results aren't where they should be, you won't have to fire me because I'm going to leave on my own."

In reality, the job was a difficult assignment and, similar to his time in Louisville, Immelt had done a good job in a tough situation. Even though reports are that he almost got fired, Immelt showed toughness and problem-solving abilities that earned favor from Welch and his peers. Nevertheless, Immelt enjoys retelling the story years later of Welch threatening his future as a lesson for all GE employees.

Immelt believes that problems can be solved and mistakes can be overcome if their occurrences are kept to a minimum. The pricing issue was one big unforeseen problem that he quickly solved. As a result, he became a better manager from the experience.

"I was a thousand times more valuable to the company, having gone through that," Immelt said. "I had 10 times more self-confidence because I knew I could work through issues of my own creation. Besides, I already knew when he chewed my butt out that I was going to turn it around."

Trial by Fire

Not only was Immelt a standout high school and collegiate athlete, but he still loves the applicable lessons learned from competition, particularly those relating to teamwork, preparation, and the value of experience. He often watches collegiate and professional sports, was regularly tuned in to broadcasts of the Beijing Olympics when not viewing them in person, and is known to apply sports analogies to business. So he viewed his experience at GE Plastics the same way he viewed his experience at GE Appliances. Difficulties faced plus problems solved typically equal success.

After the one big quarterly miss fighting inflation in plastics, Immelt began to thrive for GE on the global business playing field and never looked back, emerging by the late 1990s as one of GE's top up-and-coming executives in the running for the company's soon-to-be-vacated lead position. Because Immelt had passed the test at GE Plastics, Welch named him in 1997 as president and CEO of GE's lucrative medical systems business, praising him at the time as a "dynamic, entrepreneurial business leader."

"I took a couple of real ass chewings from Jack," says Immelt. "You learn it isn't always perfect and you learn in adversity how to react and adapt."

GE had 11 divisions and Medical Systems was one of the most important to the company because of its high global profile, high technology base, and high profit margin. But for three consecutive years before Immelt took over GE Medical Systems, division results had been flat. The business was relying upon past strengths to generate current revenues. Immelt assessed the situation and made a quick decision: GE Medical Systems would grow through commitment to finding new partners, developing new technologies, and by providing an array of quality services to the biggest customers. Years of experience by trial and error came together for Immelt as he used skills and confidence amassed on the job to ignite the division. Specifically, he began linking GE team members with customers so that each could find common, beneficial ground.

Immelt persuaded leading hospitals on miniscule budgets to replace outdated equipment with GE's new digital machines, capable of generating better images faster, and he signed up health-care giants like HCA and Premier to long-term products and services contracts. Immelt expanded GE's umbrella of services through some 60 acquisitions of complementary smaller companies, increasing GE's market share from 25 percent to 34 percent.

Under Welch, GE in the 1980s wanted only businesses that were number one or number two in the marketplace in their competitive space. The premise was that by being the best, you can charge fairly for products and services and afford to hire the top people, creating a sustainable profit machine with solid operational management. But Immelt saw the need for a different model from the number one and number two strategy. GE Medical Systems could not just acquire company leaders. In health care, they were often too expensive if they could be bought at all.

Besides, Immelt had no time to waste. He and division leaders made lists of all companies operating in GE Medical System's space, drawing lines to which ones could bolster GE's products and services offering. Even if these smaller companies were not number one or two, by being acquired, they could help GE be the best overall in the medical systems space.

Another strategy Immelt used was involving customers directly in GE's solutions strategy through information-sharing meetings. He got customers to talk about what they needed through informal sessions. Then he involved them directly in the product solution by sharing what was previously considered proprietary. Immelt also relied heavily upon technology for self-generated growth, making big bets on imaging equipment like the first digital mammogram system and the LightSpeed CT, the world's fastest CAT scan machine which paid off handsomely in revenue and profit growth.

Within three years division sales had increased by 75 percent. The division's public image had also improved as Immelt got GE Medical Systems involved in the clean up and repair of neglected public schools. And, pleasing to Welch, Immelt implemented the vaunted Six Sigma management process into Medical Systems.

Originally developed in the mid-1980s by Motorola, Six Sigma is a management strategy designed to identify and eliminate errors and defects in manufacturing and business processes. Based on principles of quality management by the likes of Edwards Deming and Walter Shewhart, drawing upon martial arts terminology like "black belt" for employees, Six Sigma is designed to work beyond the manufacturing floor, extending into all levels of an organization including the executive offices.

Welch began implementing Six Sigma at GE in the mid-1990s with good results and hoped that the strategy would become part of his leadership legacy. The fact that Immelt was growing GE Medical Systems rapidly while also effectively juggling implementation of this significant business process infrastructure only made his star shine brighter.

Ultimately, Immelt grew GE Medical Systems sales in just a few years from $3.9 billion in revenues to $7.2 billion. The primary strategy he used to achieve the growth was a first-run version of what would become a more formal companywide growth process years later under his leadership as chairman and CEO. But when he first implemented his signature plan at GE Medical Systems in the 1990s, heads inside the company were turned in attention, including the head of GE's most discerning company CEO, who adored Immelt's growth-strategy creativity. Immelt made such a quick impact, in fact, that in 1997, he made GE's list of the final eight candidates being considered to replace the legendary Welch.

By June 2000 the race to succeed Jack Welch was narrowed to a list of three finalists vying for the job. It included Immelt; Bob Nardelli, who led GE's Power Systems division to operating income of $2.8 billion from $770 million in just six years; and Jim McNerney, who led GE's Aircraft division to sales growth from $7.8 billion to $10.8 billion in four years and made it the company's most profitable segment. Both Nardelli and McNerney were different from Welch—who isn't? But their differences were not as pronounced as those of Welch and Immelt.

Consider:

- Welch was known for beautiful handwriting and sending personal notes to employees; Immelt says his handwriting is terrible, so he e-mails personal notes to employees.
- Welch raised his voice and harshly criticized employees who underperformed or made mistakes, while Immelt is more approachable and is more likely to make a point on a difficult issue with an employee with a lighthearted joke. Yet he is just as serious about the results.
- Welch would fire an employee and never look back; Immelt fires employees too, but once called a friend he let go afterward to see how he was doing amid the change.
- Welch preferred his office in Manhattan's Rockefeller Center; each month Immelt typically spends one week in his New York office, one week in his Fairfield office, and the other two weeks in GE facilities and seeing customers around the world.
- Welch, wrote one scribe, was revered, while Immelt is adored.

Differences between the two had no impact on the friendship or respect they had for one another; on the contrary. They have both professed on numerous occasions over the years an appreciation for diverging styles and mutual love and admiration for one another. If anything, Immelt's differences from Welch made him a more viable candidate for GE's top job since the company's culture can be described as having similarities of a church: the minister may change, bringing different initiatives and leadership styles, but the congregation sticks to the same ingrained, foundational guiding principles.

Consider only that GE makes products like jet engines and medical scanning devices and that each is embedded in totally separate businesses. The company has a true multibusiness platform, operating its different entities under one unifying management umbrella. For example, if the company sold its aviation business, the core of GE's foundation remains the same: management integrity and management principles designed to give return to customers, employees, and shareholders through the best possible means; a simple statement in words perhaps, but not in execution. Because, while underlying qualities like commitment to quality and the development of employees at all levels may never waver, the entity must change and evolve to maintain its edge, adapting to demands and styles of new eras and new leaders.

With so much at stake in the imminent leadership change, considering no blue chip company in the United States had ever delivered reliability and returns over two decades the way GE had, the three-man race at GE to be Welch's successor became arguably the most-watched corporate job search in history as GE's leadership role was widely considered the world's most elite corporate position.

Even though GE's practice was to promote leaders from within—all of the company's 11 previous leaders had come from internal ranks—the two not chosen for the job faced considerable personal change because Welch let all three know he expected the runners-up to leave the company once the decision was made. So each had decades of corporate job progression on the line regardless of whether or not they got Welch's job. No sense, figured Welch, letting passed-over executives get in the way of transition by hanging around, allowing employees to second-guess the final decision.

Reward for Success

Immelt says he does not recall specifically the words Welch used in telling him GE's top job was his, but he remembers getting the phone call at 5:30 on a Friday afternoon, the day after Thanksgiving. Welch had told each of the three candidates to be reachable, so Immelt anticipated the phone call.

Welch had convened a meeting of GE's board of directors by conference call that day to make a formal decision, though he had already reached his. In less than 30 minutes, deliberation by the board was complete and Welch made the call to Immelt, relaying the decision. Until that moment Immelt says he really did not know if he would get the job or not, and he was prepared for any decision. Immelt was home for the holiday when Welch called.

"I just knew I was absolutely ready (for the process) to be over," says Immelt.

When Welch called to tell Immelt he had the job, he invited him down to Palm Beach for an intimate, celebratory dinner. Welch also invited Dammerman and another GE executive, Robert Wright. Immelt says he never asked why he was chosen over the other two candidates and Welch never offered much explanation except to say later on the record that Immelt was an easy choice because he is "comfortable in his own skin."

Age might have been a tilting factor in Immelt's favor as well. Seven years younger than McNerney and eight years younger than Nardelli, Immelt could make a 20-year run as GE's leader just as Welch did while McNerney and Nardelli reasonably could not have lasted more than a decade and a half. And Welch said once that he believed his successor would need at least 10 years on the job to have a meaningful impact. Regardless, however, of why he was chosen, Immelt was amenable.

"I always felt I knew how to do this job," Immelt says. "And both Jim and Bob are extremely well qualified obviously. But if you try to put too much on paper on why the decision was made, it becomes difficult. A lot in these types of decisions are gut feeling in the end. You look at what direction the company needs to go and who is available, and you try to make sure these two things intersect."

On Sunday, two days after Immelt was notified, Welch flew to Cincinnati to meet McNerney and Albany to meet Nardelli to break the news that Immelt was chosen as GE's next chairman and CEO. McNerney recalls Welch breaking the news in memorable fashion.

They were in Cincinnati, at the airport. Rain was falling outside. Inside, a company was in the midst of metamorphosis.

"It was just the two of us," recalls McNerney. "It was foggy. Welch had a briefcase in his hand."

Among the first phone calls Immelt made after accepting the job that Thanksgiving weekend was to his father in Cincinnati, who worked for GE as a middle-level manager for almost four decades. Immelt recalls his father's excitement at the news as one of his prouder moments. Then, he says, his father gave a directive, urging him to "do something about the pension" in a half-joking tone.

Somewhat surprisingly, since the search for Welch's successor was so closely followed, the news did not break publicly over the holiday weekend. Not until Welch and Immelt appeared jointly, speaking casually and comfortably in open collared shirts and sports jackets at a news conference that Monday morning from NBC Studios at Rockefeller Center did anyone outside the inner circle and family members know about Immelt's anointing.

American business was traveling a rocky road at the time with the crashing of the dot-com bubble and the apparent end of the raging bull market which helped in part fuel GE's remarkable stock price run in the 1990s. To allow for a smooth transition in the turbulent times and to manage the company's attempted purchase of Honeywell, Welch remained officially in office once the decision was made. Thus, in early 2001, Immelt was effectively GE's chief operating officer, while Welch focused on his role as chairman and the attempted purchase of Honeywell.

Assumption might be that Welch and Immelt strategized together, planning the company's future, but that did not often happen. Welch wanted the Honeywell deal to be his last great achievement, and he worked hard at making it happen though a European Union commission got in the way, blocking the sale based on antitrust concerns. With the Honeywell deal requiring his time, Welch stepped back from operations, turning over most leadership decisions to Immelt.

"We purposefully did not spend time plotting the next five to ten years," Immelt says of his last months on the job with Welch. "We knew the world would change, the company would be different. I had in my mind direction for the twenty-first century, but Jack was just there with moral support."

Not once, Immelt says, did he question whether he was prepared and able to lead GE.

The biggest challenge, he figured, was overcoming the view of GE which often placed Welch at the forefront, despite the fact that the company with more than 300,000 employees was known for its depth in leadership far beyond the CEO's office.

"Everybody at GE thinks they work for Jack; every customer of GE thinks they buy from Jack; every political person thinks they deal with Jack," said Immelt in 2001.

Welch remained on the job a bit longer than anticipated because of the company's attempted purchase of Honeywell and the turbulence of the markets, but he reached a decision to retire at the end of the work day on September 7, 2001, following a company board meeting. On that day, Welch walked away with finality from the company he had led with vigor for just more than two decades. For Immelt, the transition presented opportunity. He knew the company needed to change. For years GE had ridden hard several prized profitable divisions like plastics and appliances to fuel extraordinary sales and profits growth. He knew, however, by the end of Welch's term that what worked well for the former chairman and CEO would not suffice for the future.

"They were like marathon runners," Immelt says years later in reflection over GE divisions that were slowing in growth near the turn of the century. "They ran a great race, but they passed out over the finish line."

But the 45-year-old Immelt relished the challenge in retooling the company and was full of enthusiasm on his first day in the office minus Welch, ready to smoothly begin GE's next generation of leadership.

By all standards, he did have a really good day.

The calendar read September 10, 2001.

Congratulatory phone calls poured in.

A feature story on Immelt ran in *Time* magazine under the headline "Jack Who?"

And the company's stock closed that day at a split-adjusted price of $32.86, flirting with an all-time high in market capitalization.

To make sure that GE's vaunted customer base remained confident and loyal during the leadership transition, Immelt had traveled the world since he was chosen to replace Welch, making sure that he personally transferred key relationships. Nothing would change in his new assigning. So on September 10, he boarded the company jet, traveling to Seattle for a customer meeting.

Immelt made the trip with a broad confidence that the transition from Welch had gone better than he could have imagined. GE had effectively survived the crashing of the technology stocks the year before and smoothly made the closely watched switch from Welch to Immelt. Distractions behind, he could now go about the job of reshaping the company for its next generation of business.

CHAPTER 3

STRENGTH IN CRISIS

"This is not just a job. This is a passion. This is my life."

—JEFF IMMELT

Most big corporations move and change at the pace of a
bureaucratic crawl, but after GE emerged from the
1990s, the company was as nimble as any giant can be. Immelt
planned in his first days, weeks, and months in the leadership
job to take advantage of the agility, putting existing processes
to work while introducing new ones to quickly move the entity
into the future. The problem, however, is that one never knows
exactly what the future holds.

Just like that, with the rising of the sun and the onset of
tragic, world-altering events on September 11, 2001, everything changed; optimism turned to despair, life became death,
and firm foundations trembled. People around the world were
shaken, concerned about the future, and wondering how life
and business might change.

What a difference one day can make.

The World Changed

GE's new chairman and CEO awakened early on the West Coast in the morning of September 11, 2001, for his usual exercise routine before work. He found out after turning on the television from his Seattle hotel room that events three time zones away were changing the world and the stance of his company before his eyes. Since GE owns the television network NBC, Immelt was naturally tuned there for the breaking news, but the connection for him and his company ran much deeper than that.

Before selling the last piece of its insurance business in 2005, GE was a significant player in the casualty and loss business, particularly on the reinsurance side, backing such large entities as New York's World Trade Center. And one of GE's most lucrative and reliable businesses is aviation, a top supplier of jet engines in the world. Not to mention that two GE employees were among the thousands who died that morning.

Immelt joined the millions of people moved to the point of pall and uneasiness when the tragic events unfolded that day. In Seattle, Immelt was traveling with a laptop computer, but he could not get through company network firewalls to reach GE's employee intranet. So he made a few phone calls and found a local GE sales office. The space was cramped, little more than a handful of cubicles and a small break room, but Immelt went to work, assessing the situation, working phones and fax machine to collect information and pass along instructions.

He made a quick decision to delay a scheduled investors meeting for September 16, but by only two days, because he wanted to show the company's strength in the face of adversity.

He sent as many GE electrical power generators as possible to the World Trade Center site, and he stuck to his rule number one as leader in a crisis: be visible. GE also sent out its first all-employee e-mail that day and sent its second one several days later. Still, Immelt admits that he was uncharacteristically rattled by the enormity of the events. Understandably so, since few CEOs could have felt the diversified weight of the world from a business perspective the way Immelt did that fateful day.

Some companies suffered more human tragedy. Some companies lost more money from the events. But as the leader of the world's largest corporate conglomerate, Immelt had a unique 9/11 perspective. Consider only that among the first phone calls New York Mayor Rudi Giuliani received that day was from Immelt, who offered assurance that GE would offer support and send a strong message to the markets that the company would not be deterred. Replacing Jack Welch was no longer Jeff Immelt's biggest concern.

GE's insurance business took a $600 million hit that day, and the orders for the company's jet engines declined with ensuing turmoil in the airline industry. Worsening the situation for GE was the company's exposure in financing capital purchases for many airlines through GE Capital and the fact that GE's entertainment division lost millions in revenue to lost commercial time in covering 9/11 on networks NBC, MSNBC, and CNBC. Yet two days after the attack Giuliani announced that Immelt committed $10 million on behalf of GE to aid families of victims including those of service personnel.

"Let's categorize September 11 as an amazing tragedy, just an unbelievable, unspeakable tragedy," said Immelt. "It had an impact on the airline industry and the tourism industry and the insurance industry. But this economy was in recession on September 10. This economy started getting worse in August of 2000. It was accelerating in terms of getting in a recessionary mode. And September 11 just made it tougher."

Determined to not let the events derail the company, even temporarily, Immelt held the planned investors meeting two days later. He was working hard through phone calls and public relations efforts to ensure the world that GE was on solid ground, even with diminished prospects resulting from 9/11 and the slowing economy. But when the New York Stock Exchange reopened on September 17 for the first time since the terrorist attacks, GE's stock took a hard hit along with other stalwarts, closing down by more than 11 percent.

The American economy was already in the early stages of recession, and imminent slowing caused by fear and damage from the terrorist attacks would weigh on all companies, even a blue-chip bull like GE. In the following days, GE's stock price continued to sink, losing almost $80 billion in market capitalization, yet Immelt was telling everyone on Wall Street who would listen that he was trying to buy all shares of the company's stock he could in support and that he had complete confidence in the resiliency of the 300,000 plus workers employed by GE.

Fallout from Enron

At the same time, GE was being affected by the unfolding Enron scandal. For six consecutive years at the close of the twentieth century, Houston, Texas–based energy conglomerate

Enron was named the most innovative company in the United States by leading business publications. Wall Street had the same admiration for the energy company, which by 2000 was the world leader in electricity, natural gas, and other related products and services with stated revenues of $111 billion. Enron had soared to remarkable growth in the 1990s by exploiting U.S. deregulation of the sale of electricity and had become a Wall Street darling mentioned in the same breath by many investors as a stalwart like GE.

However, one month before the events of 9/11, warning signs emerged from Enron that the company had serious foundational problems. Jeffrey Skilling had abruptly resigned in August 2001 as company CEO. He had been on the job just six months, and, in that time, had unloaded some 450,000 shares for more than $30 million in proceeds. Wall Street was alarmed, and journalists began to question the strength and viability of Enron.

Up to that point, the issue was lack of disclosure from Enron, and as more questions were asked, the more Enron chairman Kenneth Lay and key financial personnel clammed up. Even some of the most experienced analysts could not decipher Enron's complicated bookkeeping, and the company was providing no answers, only responding with more superficial assurances. Then 9/11 occurred, momentarily stealing headlines and attention. Other Enron-trouble distracting headlines came into play as well, like the imminence of the United States going to war to fight terrorist regimes and the anthrax attack in October 2001 at NBC, the media company owned by GE. (An assistant to news anchor Tom Brokaw tested positive to exposure after handling a letter sent to her boss, and vulnerability continued to become reality.)

Within a month, however, Enron was back in the news as what seemed to be a case of distorted math and cloudy reporting became a full-fledged financial scam, the size of which U.S. investors had never before seen. Enron was using deregulation to allow it to play in energy as financier of natural resources, and the scheme was deeply flawed. With investor confidence already shaken, the realization that Enron was little more than a corporate shell game concealing losses and falsely inflating revenues and profits began to rub off on the stock market on respected companies like GE, which had diversified business models, regardless of whether they had done anything wrong or not.

Enron's stock price evaporated to almost nothing, the company filed for bankruptcy, and its management faced criminal charges. GE, on the other hand, had very little exposure to Enron compared to other companies heavily into corporate finance, including Citicorp and JPMorgan Chase. But the collateral damage to the company's stock price was measurable merely by default—the market did not trust big business. By the end of the year, GE shareholders had seen a value erosion of 16 percent, slightly more than the average of the Standard & Poor's 500, despite the fact that company earnings increased to a record $14.1 billion, an 11 percent increase, while the S&P average earnings declined by more than 20 percent.

Seven years later Immelt still becomes animated when recalling the difficult chain of events he encountered as he followed Jack Welch into the leadership of GE.

"9/11 had a big impact," says Immelt, speaking from his Fairfield office in a pressed white shirt with sleeves rolled halfway up his arms, "but there were three things that really came together at that time in such a big way. One, you had the end of the bubble economy and the bursting of the dot-coms. Two, you had 9/11 which caused us all to ask how the U.S. fit into the larger world. Three, you had Enron. When that happened, every (American) CEO became a crook.

"I was caught right in the middle of all of them," Immelt says, raising both hands for effect.

If those cataclysmic financial market–impacting events were not enough, by 2002 the world learned that conglomerate Tyco was under stress, losing billions. Tyco chairman and CEO Dennis Kozlowski resigned under pressure for taking exorbitant pay and on-the-job perks involving hundreds of millions of dollars. Kozlowski ultimately went to prison for his deeds and, though completely uninvolved, Immelt and GE paid a marketplace price again.

In early 2002, Immelt had mentioned Kozlowski and Tyco to a reporter at *BusinessWeek* when asked what companies were building a business model similar to that of GE. Immelt also mentioned Jean-Marie Messier, who was the CEO of the global media giant Vivendi, as a business executive he admired. Like Kozlowski, Messier took a fall for workplace greed in 2002, having used corporate funds to buy a New York apartment for $17.5 million before he was ousted.

Immelt said months later that he regretted using the names of Kozlowski and Messier in his interview response, just as he regretted not focusing more quickly on the internal aspects of GE. As a result, he felt the need to soothe and assuage by assurances and tactics like more financial transparency to show that the company was not Enron or Tyco. Investors, Immelt said, "read a lot into every change" and he admits could have, should have "moved faster" in building GE's business models that he had planned for the twenty-first century in spite of the disruptions.

But the market just was not trusting anymore, even in respect to old reliable. Where Jack Welch had begun his tenure under difficult conditions in 1981, he ended his career riding more than a decade of tailwinds. Immelt, however, was flying after his first days in office straight into stiff headwinds that never seemed to let up.

Says Immelt: "I was a rookie CEO ... following the most famous guy in history. But the times were extremely different for my predecessor. The late 1990s was about every tree growing to the sky and admiration of CEOs."

Immelt was frankly glad to see his first year on the job come to a close. Company revenues were flat as a result of the recessionary environment, and earnings growth was minimal, though Immelt believes they did a good job just maintaining growth right after 9/11.

"The first year was tougher than I could imagine. You had 9/11, Enron, and the recession. The way CEOs and companies were viewed changed 180 degrees in 15 minutes."

CHAPTER 4

APPEARANCES CAN BE DECEIVING

"I think longevity is a function of two things. It's a function of performance and your own ability to reinvent yourself."

—JEFF IMMELT

W hat seemed like short-term trouble for GE with the implosion of Enron turned out to be a long-term blessing in disguise.

Still today Immelt cringes at the mention of Enron's novelistic downfall because of the collateral damage it inflicted. Jobs were lost. Retirement accounts were obliterated. Who can scoff at that? But the trite saying that every cloud has a silver lining certainly applies to Jeff Immelt and GE in regard to Enron.

Call it a case of calculated opportunity paying big dividends.

Since Jack Welch became GE's chairman and CEO in 1981, the company had prospered from an acquisitions strategy. But the difference in GE and companies like Enron, Tyco, and Vivendi, according to Immelt, is a matter of culture. GE makes the same big bets through acquisition and investment as those companies did, seeking handsome payoffs for investors, but GE does so with decidedly more conservative processes and disposition. Purchases are made only through careful study, and, once GE has new businesses in hand, the company's management is better equipped to run, grow, and profit from the acquisition.

GE is not perfect in its acquisitions record, of course. Sometimes the company misses, like when its insurance business turned out to be more burden than boost or when a large investment in retailer Montgomery Ward backfired in a big way. Company subsidiary GE Capital was heavily vested in the retailer, which was once one of the largest in the United States, with more than 400 stores nationally before filing for bankruptcy in 1997.

But GE has scored big with most of its acquisitions and big-bet strategies. Perhaps none illustrates this better than what the company purchased from Enron during Immelt's first year on the job as company chairman and CEO. For years GE had studied the viability of the wind business through its energy division and Global Research Center in Niskayuna, New York.

Wind Power

Among the company's champions for wind were Jim Lyons, who is now retired but was serving as chief engineer for electronics and energy conversion at GE Global Research, and Mark Little, a company director now leading the research center who was vice president of GE Energy's power generation segment at the time. Lyons holds a doctoral degree from Cornell University he earned in 1984, and his Ph.D. thesis was on variable speed wind turbine generators. As an engineer at GE during a career spanning more than 30 years, Lyons was a corporate champion for renewable energy long before the subject became a hot global topic. The benefits and corporate viability of wind power generation was Lyons' passion, and he had a keen listener in Little who not only understood the concept but helped fund and foster study of the wind business.

Little holds three degrees in mechanical engineering, including a Ph.D., and, like Lyons, he began a career with GE Energy in the 1970s, working as an engineer in Schenectady. Among Little's career assignments was the company's gas turbine business, number one in its space. Little became manager, and it was tough, he says because technical problems surfaced, costing the company big money in recalls and repairs. Little had to explain to Jack Welch what was going on.

"[Welch] said, 'We want them to say, lousy product, but the best company to have a problem with is GE,'" recalls Little.

Later in his career, Little ran business development for GE Energy, one of the company's larger businesses, giving him a unique role for the company, serving as liaison between the creative and business sides of the company. You can bring good ideas to life, but if they can't make money, they don't have a place in a growth– and bottom-line–oriented company like GE. Even a promising renewable energy initiative like wind power generation must be sustainable and profitable to justify heavy investment.

Wind made a lot of sense for GE, however, according to the persistent argument by Lyons. The company held vast proprietary knowledge which applied to wind from its gas-powered turbines business, and GE made some of the lightest and best propeller blades for aircraft engines. GE was also one of the world's most respected companies with well-established key relationships throughout the world, increasing chances of success with a new global energy initiative.

Convinced they had a new business winner, Little and Lyons went to Jack Welch in the late 1990s and made a pitch.

"We need to be in the wind business," Little said.

No, said Welch, rather emphatically.

The model was largely based on the promise that the world would one day require vast amounts of renewable energy alternatives like wind. While nobody doubted that this would eventually occur, rolling the dice on such an expensive proposition made little sense to Welch. One day into the future as a potential payoff was not good enough for a company called to meet and exceed shareholder expectations on a quarterly basis.

"When Jack was CEO," says Little, "we did not get a warm reaction. He did not see wind as a serious business."

Enron's Kenneth Lay did, however.

The former Enron CEO had already made a sizable move into wind. Lay was intrigued by the concept because he understood that environmental initiatives like wind-generated energy represented unlimited opportunity for the company, whereas other, more traditional energy formats like oil, gas, and coal were tightly controlled by long-standing corporate interests. So typically, Enron made money in energy only through resell or finance.

Green initiatives were untapped and uncontrolled, and growth therefore held exponential promise, according to Lay.

Government subsidies intended to foster alternative energy generation supported wind energy initiatives and made business prospects more intriguing. Besides, renewable energy initiatives looked good on an annual report summary, even in the gas-guzzling 1990s.

GE has been far more conservative at its corporate core than Enron ever was on its best day, history reveals, so the company's position at the time is easily explained. If the wind business ever panned out, GE could simply afford to make an acquisition. In the meantime, somebody else should do the money-losing experimentation.

And that is exactly what Enron did under Lay, delving deeply considering the limited marketplace for wind energy which existed at the time. Wind was the fastest-growing energy technology globally in the late 1990s, but it still met less than 5 percent of demand. Also, system infrastructure costs were high, and reliability was an issue as wind speeds vary constantly and technology was in the infancy stage. Enron, however, had invested hundreds of millions of dollars in establishing its wind business, creating a manufacturing presence in four countries which held the natural disposition and growth opportunities for the windmill structures, including Germany, the Netherlands, Spain, and the United States. Enron also established a sales presence in a half dozen other countries where the environmental initiative made sense.

Meanwhile, GE sat on the sidelines, continuing to study business feasibility. Lyons and Little were relentless in seeking GE's participation. By the dawn of the new millennium, wind was catching on as government entities increasingly recognized that the twenty-first century called for renewable energy. Incentives in Germany, the United States, and Spain almost doubled wind generation capacity in 1999 and 2000, and GE Energy was ready to make a substantial leap. Domestically, the state of Texas instituted a mandate calling for more renewable energy sources, and Minnesota and Iowa began subsidizing wind.

Welch was still with the company in early 2001 when Little made another visit to pitch the company's leadership on a sizable investment in the wind business, but Immelt had effectively taken over the role of GE's operational leader.

"They suited me up to go see the new guy, Jeff," says Little.

Previously, Little struck out pitching the wind business to Welch. But demand for wind was growing, and the energy division felt that it had a better grasp of technology and customers in the space. GE Energy was one of the parent company's largest and most productive components, so Little's voice was heard, loud and clear. Little's impassioned plea was fraught with promise of potential. Immelt was not initially moved to the point of action, however, viewing the lofty price tag for start-up against realistic returns on investment.

"I said, 'This is a Hula Hoop, a whack job,'" recalls Immelt, laughing.

He sent Little and Lyons back to the drawing board.

"Go back and do more homework," he said.

"Show me the conservative anticipated growth rate and how we can manage the business and make money and come back."

"Mark kept pitching," says Immelt. "Sometimes when you are the CEO, you play the role of the Wizard of Oz. You say, 'Bring me the broom of the Wicked Witch of the West. Prove to me she exists.' Well, they did.

"Simultaneously I looked at the cost of entry," says Immelt. "It was still too expensive."

Such careful consideration is part of the analysis process for GE, which, as one of the world's largest companies in the world in market capitalization and borrowing ability, can acquire almost any company it wants on a whim. Instead, GE moves carefully through fact-finding and information-sharing to invest wisely in new businesses. Enron had jumped, but the company was not making money on wind; Enron was merely making marketplace presence headway. Enron's turbines were clunky, and often unreliable contracts were locked into set pricing for too long, thus limiting profit potential.

But Little and Lyons were not backing down, believing in the growth and profit prospects of wind energy, not to mention the environmental benefits of power generation that relied upon a free and nonpolluting source. Wind energy does not release greenhouse gases associated with global warming, and wind presumably is inexhaustible though it can be unpredictable. For GE, the break came when Enron spiraled into trouble at the end of 2001. By the time the company filed for bankruptcy, little of value was left, yet GE found the opportunity it had been looking for.

"Mark comes back to me," recalls Immelt. "He says, 'If we buy this from Enron, we can probably get it for $250 million.' I told him to go for it. That seemed like a good price of entry."

Enron's wind division was a world leader in the space, with contracts across several continents and growing orders for its wind turbines which generated electricity from nature's breath.

But the business was in its infancy, plagued with problems, and devoid of the quality management needed to be a growth engine for a true blue-chip corporation. On the manufacturing side, Enron's products had, according to Immelt, "lousy design" and were literally "breaking in the field," and sales were disconnected from longer-term business objectives. Enron's wind division was profitable by 2001, earning money on revenues which had grown to $800 million from just $50 million four years before, but the business's foundation was not nearly as strong as GE wanted it to be.

"[Enron's wind business] was a very broken model that took us three years to fix," says Immelt. "GE has earned the trust of the customers, and we already had relationships with many. They know we can lean into a deep bench and take the time to make it right."

GE had to pay more for Enron's wind business than originally expected, but when GE emerged from Enron's bankruptcy court in April 2002 as the winner of the court auction at a price of $358 million, the company nabbed what would become one of its most profitable and important businesses of the early twenty-first century.

"We bought this crappy little wind business ... when wind was nothing but a Hula Hoop—25 cents a kilowatt hour, nothing but a Hula Hoop," Immelt told business school students during a November 2007 lecture at Cornell University, which was simultaneously broadcast to students at five other universities. "Now it's 6 cents a kilowatt hour because we've industrialized it. So, you know ... big companies take a lot of heat, some of it deservedly so for being short termers on long-term things like that. But if you want to see history, I just won't concede any of it has to happen in Silicon Valley in somebody's garage. I think we can do a lot better, a lot more effectively and a lot more efficiently inside our company."

Applying its financial, management, research, and engineering muscle, GE established its wind energy business in May 2002, rebuilding the foundation started by Enron from the ground up.

John Rice, who now serves as vice chairman of GE and oversees one of four company divisions as president and CEO of GE Technology Infrastructure, was the head of GE Energy from 2000 to 2005 and behind the charge to get the company into the wind business. But even though he pushed the pitches to Welch and Immelt for a start-up, he believes in the end it was all part of a necessary process leading to the right destination. GE did not make a move earlier because "the timing was not right."

"If we had invested in wind in 1995," says Rice, "we probably would have been out of it by 1998 because the market was not big enough, and the technology was not mature enough."

But when Enron's unit became available in 2001, Rice says, GE "had a team of people ready to jump in."

"In that type of (bankruptcy court) situation," says Rice, "you often have several bidders, and you go back and forth presenting information until one person has the last bid, so you have to do your homework. We don't do hostile takeovers, so we are paced sometimes by need to have a willing seller. You try to pick the right time to get in. We had done our homework and ended up winning the bid.

"We wish we could have bought two."

Cross-Pollination Is Key to Success

Immediately, GE became a force in wind, making improvements in all aspects from product design to contract structure. Because GE had managed to purchase the growing business at such a deep discount, the company could invest generously without incurring the billions it would have spent with a wind business start-up. And because GE is a diversified company with global girth, the energy division was able to work cross-company and cross-continentally to find solutions. GE's culture has long emanated from the strength of its beating heart, found at the company's leadership training center in Crotonville, New York.

Founded in 1956, the John F. Welch Leadership Development Center (the facility was renamed upon Welch's retirement in 2001) was the first of its kind in the world—a 53-acre learning campus designed to foster cross-company and cross-discipline creativity and innovation. Located just 30 miles outside of Manhattan, the facility opened as a traditional classroom teaching center for GE employees, but it evolved considerably under Welch. He saw the need after taking the company's leadership position in 1981 to make Crotonville a place of both motivation and cultivation for GE.

With meandering paths in an equalizing environment which provides name tags and rooms of the same size to all participants regardless of their employment level, the center brings employees of all disciplines to one place so together they can find the common good and goals—the culture. Welch established the center as a centerpiece for driving change through the organization and pushing employees to perform, while

Immelt continued that tradition but added the element of bringing customers to Crotonville to join collaboration. The result is a company that can easily work beyond its boundaries without many of the debilitating proprietary issues that plague corporations.

That is not to say GE does not experience internal turf battles. Naturally, these occur from time to time, but because an employee from aviation, for instance, is often paired at Crotonville over the span of a three-week, on-site course with an employee from finance, the culture learns how to quickly and easily cross barriers for mutual benefit. Their businesses may have seemingly little to nothing in common, but they are taught to reach beyond boundaries.

The benefits of this cross-company teamwork culture have been evident in the evolution of GE's wind business. Rice had a team assembled and ready to go upon the company's winning the Enron wind bid. Lyons led the technologies effort, drawing upon GE engineering talent from around the world, regardless of discipline. In aviation, he found material experts familiar with lighter-weight products for turbine blades. In GE's rail business, Lyons used experts who know how to make gearing systems operate at peak efficiency. In the United States and Germany he put industrial designers to work, while in places like Bangalore and Shanghai he found company researchers to build analytical models and conduct high-end simulations of wind turbines in use, revealing improvements needed and progress made.

Rice, meanwhile, went about changing the business model from what Enron had used. The practice, he said, was to sign customers buying wind turbines to long-term contracts with no price escalation. When the price of steel and other raw materials went up by as much as 50 percent just after GE bought the business, the cost of a wind turbine doubled and GE was locked into the contracts it inherited in the bankruptcy purchase. The situation was similar to what Immelt faced years before at GE Plastics when prices soared and existing contracts held the company back. As a result GE lost money two of its first three years in the wind business.

But the problem was fixed when GE changed to flexible pricing contracts, and the market for wind turbines took off. Only 7 states had implemented renewable energy standards in 2000. This increased to 29 in 2008. Those factors, combined with GE's improvements in the product and its position with government entities as a trusted and reliable business partner contributed to a growth explosion in the wind business.

"All of the problems (with Enron's business) were things we knew we would be able to fix," says Rice. "We believed in the size of the market, but we did not predict that so many states would take matters into their own hands as quickly as they did."

By 2005, just three years after GE entered the wind business, revenues were up by more than 300 percent, and in 2008 they exceeded $6 billion with orders extending into 2010, beyond expiration of a U.S. tax credit for new wind turbine construction.

"We paid approximately $300 million for the wind business, and revenues in 2008 will be almost 20 times that," says Rice. "Obviously, wind has been hugely successful. A combination of things contributed to this success, including good old-fashioned hard work and being in the right place at the right time. You have to have an element of luck. The market was turning in our favor.

"But you do create much of your luck."

For Immelt, reflection on GE's much-debated entry into the wind business and its ultimate success with it show the company's culture is at work. Welch said no because he did not like the model. Immelt said no originally because he worried about short-term profitability versus the investment needed to fund a start-up. But ultimately he approved the purchase when GE found an established wind business in the bargain bin of bankruptcy court. Throughout the process, though, GE was building knowledge through research so that when opportunity came, the company could ably seize upon it.

"Now I brag and say, 'That was my idea,'" says Immelt, laughing. "But for a company like GE, decisions like this are a process. We plant the seeds. We don't have to be right all the time. But we study. And when we feel the time is right, we go. We don't follow a whim or a trend; we go because the timing and the product and the price is right."

Now, such careful and planned cultivation of innovation is part of the new GE way—Immelt's commitment to develop long-term plans and products for the company.

CHAPTER 5

UNDERSTAND CONTEXT

"Leadership is about resiliency. It is about picking up after setbacks and keeping going."

—JEFF IMMELT

Execution in business most often determines results, but perceived momentum more often determines the marketplace value of a company.

Few corporate leaders know this better than GE's Jeff Immelt, who in just more than 12 months on the job as chairman and CEO watched his company's stock price lose almost half its value despite quantifiable progress in difficult times. The headwind that began on September 11, 2001, was not letting up. The resistance suggested that the law of averages was finally catching up with GE and that all the goodwill that gave the company and its stock price one benefit of the doubt after another in the 1990s was running in reverse.

Immelt understands that he inherited a company that in 2001 was trading at a price-to-earnings multiple of 35 times while the average of the Standard & Poor's 500 was just 25. Even before 9/11, he faced a stiff challenge because of his succession. Now, the headwind was gaining strength. Analysts did not seem to care that GE plucked the wind business from the bankrupt energy giant Enron or that GE was holding up relatively well in the slowing economy, maintaining respectable profitability and growth. And once challenges of his first year are added in, one can quickly understand Immelt's initial challenge at keeping the stock price up.

But the story on how GE, the former world business leader in market capitalization, dropped from a high of nearly $40 a share in 2001 to a price of just $22 a share in October 2002 was only partially told in the aftermath of Enron and 9/11. GE was a well-established blue-chip company with a time-tested reputation of reliability and trust, but the external pendulum continued swinging in 2002 far to the negative side.

The financial community was just accepting the downfall of Enron when WorldCom, one of the world's largest communications companies, emerged publicly as having perpetuated fraud. Under the leadership of CEO Bernie Ebbers, a Sunday school-teaching, blue jeans and cowboy-boot-wearing company founder who professed under oath to know little about technology, engineering, and accounting, Mississippi-based WorldCom became the world leader in communications in terms of girth in 1998 when the company officially merged with MCI, becoming MCI WorldCom.

But the rise to the top was short-lived as, throughout most of 2001 and continuing into the spring of 2002, MCI WorldCom's stock price dropped precipitously. Ebbers was ousted in April 2002, the company in July 2002 filed the largest bankruptcy ever in the United States (a distinction which stood until Lehman Brothers filed for bankruptcy protection in 2008), and

Ebbers and others including the company's CFO and controller were convicted of accounting fraud for inflating assets over a period of several years by more than $11 billion. As with shareholders of Enron and Tyco, MCI WorldCom investors were left holding stock worth almost nothing. And even though GE held a track record dating back to its founding in the 1800s, its shareholders suffered from increased corporate scrutiny and suspicion as well.

"I never had a fear about the company, but I would say to myself, 'My God, what else can happen next?'" said Immelt. "Because when you run a company the size of GE, sometimes there's collateral damage from an Enron or a WorldCom."

Without a doubt, GE experienced collateral damage from a shareholder perspective. One such direct hit occurred in March 2002 when prominent money manager Bill Gross of PIMCO publicly questioned the company's credit and credibility. His report came out on a Monday, the same day that Immelt and GE had 120 analysts and investors in Crotonville for a share-and-tell type of meeting. "We talked about acquisitions—how many we do and how we do them—the capital structure," Immelt said at the time.

PIMCO was invited, he said, but did not show. Gross, instead, publicly stole the show. Joining the suspicious tone mounting against Wall Street's biggest companies, particularly those involved in a steady stream of business acquisitions, Gross suggested that dating back to the Jack Welch era, GE had merely purchased its vaunted growth and was overexposed in the credit market by not having sufficient bank backing for commercial paper issued through its lending arm, GE Capital.

"It grows earnings not so much by the brilliance of management or the diversity of their operations, as Welch and Immelt claim, but through the acquisition of companies—more than 100 companies in each of the last five years—using high-powered, high (price/earnings) multiple GE stock or cheap near-Treasury bill-yielding commercial paper," Gross said.

GE's stock dropped by 6 percent as a result of the comments, and, while Immelt says he did not respond to the comments specifically, he did have the head of GE Capital contact Gross to say that the company was absolutely not buying its way to growth. The company also released a press statement reiterating its positions in sharp contrast to Gross's allegations. And Immelt said that as a result of the tempestuous environment changes that were already underway at GE, it was his intention to become more transparent in information and reporting.

Welch was sometimes criticized for shielding specific information through the diversified company's vast businesses. With financial services contributing more than 40 percent of revenues at a company grossing well over $130 billion in annual revenue, complete transparency becomes a challenge. Yet in 2002, Immelt and GE began providing more information to investors and ratings companies than ever before.

"The week of Gross's article, we won six investor awards," said Immelt at the time. "Investors are customers, so you listen to what's on their minds. We have nothing fundamentally in the company to hide. If I think doing more is going to help our customers feel better, then we ought to do it. As we did analyst meetings last year, we started giving out charts. As we were putting together the (2002) annual report, we decided to put in more information. We've had more communication with our investors than ever before. It's just a growing emphasis."

GE's reliance on its hefty financing business, which, dating back to its consumer financing of refrigerators in the Great Depression, has fueled parent-company revenues, contributing billions in profits. But the company was also taken to task about its overall business when the first quarter earnings report in 2002 was filed, showing flat revenues over the same period of a year before. Profit also dropped for the first time in seven years, resulting in a one-day stock price decline of more than 9 percent.

Later in the year, the company lowered its earnings guidance for an upcoming quarter, doing the same thing again in 2003 as growth at the energy unit, one of the company's strongest profit centers at the time, was slowing in the faltering economy. And news in 2002 that the Securities and Exchange Commission was looking into Welch's retirement package, structured in his contract in 1996, which included use of a New York apartment for life, use of a company airplane, and country club memberships after he left office, came at a bad time considering the public's watchful eye on big corporations and executive pay following Enron and MCI WorldCom.

In response, GE's stock price had fallen to $22 in October 2002 despite the fact that the company in most respects was doing everything right in a recessionary environment. Some mistakes were made, but they were minor in the broad scheme of the times, particularly considering the fact that GE posted a record $15.1 billion in earnings in 2002, a 7 percent increase over 2001, during a period when MCI WorldCom and Enron vaporized. Immelt was learning the hard way that in global markets, a company's stock price is often directly influenced by the direction of prevailing external winds.

"I think it is one of those things you cannot give speeches about," Immelt said in 2003, after being named man of the year by the *Financial Times* of London. "The better thing I can do is lead by example ... I am just convinced that over time, as people see more and learn more, they are going to see that business people like their companies, that these jobs are honors, and we treat them that way. I do not blame anybody for being cynical right now and when you are at the peak of cynicism only actions and time will solve it."

Maintain Perspective

Ask Immelt about the company's stock price today, and he quickly reacts. He does not hide frustration that in his first seven years on the job the company's revenues, net earnings, and net earnings per share had each increased by more than 60 percent while the stock price was beaten to near a single digit price-to-earnings multiple. Sitting at a conference table in his Fairfield, Connecticut, office, Immelt is relaxed in conversation until asked about the company's stock price. His wavy hair has more gray than it once did, undoubtedly in part the result of the ongoing battle with the company's share price, dating back to his first days in office and continuing through the financial meltdown in 2008.

"Yes it frustrates me," he says, leaning in at attention. "I definitely feel that way. You want the gratification of saying you had a stock price to match your results, but you can only control what you are doing. It makes me angry, but you have to step back."

The best response is to step back and take a long-term view, just as GE has done for so many years, says Immelt. When he took over the reins of the company, GE's culture was well established, with both a short-term and long-term focus. Wall Street, however, often made more of GE's short-term results because Jack Welch was heralded for most of his leadership tenure for an ability to push and prod lieutenants to stretch beyond set goals in each and every quarter. The company's stock price soared in response. By 2000, GE traded at a price-to-earnings multiple of more than 37, well above the S&P index average of 28, which occurred at the end of the big Wall Street bull market run of the 1990s when the Dow Jones Industrial average skyrocketed from a high of 5,023 points in 1995 to its first-ever close above 11,000 points in 1999.

Behind the scenes, however, Welch orchestrated long-term planning and execution, removing layers of bureaucracy to make the company more nimble and implementing human resource processes to drive change so the company could evolve. He argued that the company must win today, but also be better in the future, and built a company over two decades run by leaders cultivated as revolutionaries, able to wake up the organization, quickly moving it forward and into the future. Thus the expectation and encouragement when he retired and turned the leadership position over to Immelt was that the long-term evolutionary process would continue. Some once-robust businesses had matured, Wall Street had already obtained well-rewarded results, the world was changing, and GE was in need of a makeover.

"At the time our stock sold at a premium valuation," says Immelt. "Our portfolio was in tough shape. Insurance was in its last great year, and plastics was in its last great year. We had to do some significant retooling."

But GE's business mix was not all that needed changing. Immelt realized after his first year on the job that he and GE faced a decidedly different marketplace in the early twenty-first century from what had been experienced in the decade before. No longer could GE beat analyst earnings projects by a few pennies and see the stock leap forward in response. Meeting or exceeding quarterly earnings expectations became more a matter of maintaining credibility amid the abounding Wall Street cynicism. And no longer should GE investors expect announcements of a billion dollar manufacturing contract or high ratings for a new NBC hit television show to send the stock skyward on a whim. A blue-chip stock like GE's is to have and to hold, says Immelt.

"You have to back off and look at a 30-year stock chart," says Immelt, during an interview in September 2008, before the market's financial crisis crash. "If you invested money 10 years ago, you had a 10 percent return. Ten years before that, the same thing and 10 years before that, the same thing. Over time, you work your way through these trends (with a trusted company)."

Immelt argues that the price-to-earnings ratio of the company was 40 when he took over while by 2008 it was down to 11. He notes that GE earned roughly $11 billion per year at the time and now earns about $21 billion. "So it's not like we've gone backwards in any way. Our revenue is higher. Our earnings were higher. Our cash flow is stronger. Our returns were improving. So you have to trust that ultimately these get viewed positively by investors."

Fortunately, says Immelt, the longer-term focus with acute attention to short-term results was a significant part of the company's culture before the big Wall Street bull run of the 1990s. He points out that dating back to the days of Edison, GE was viewed by investors almost solely for the longer term with innovation being a driving factor. He's not big into chasing the shortest-term trends anyway and once noted to a group of business school students that two members of his graduating class went to work for GE while 18 went to work for a company named Atari, asking, "Anybody ever hear of Atari today?"

So when the world changed so dramatically after his first year on the job, he understood more clearly that the company had to continue its internal focus on short-term results but the company had to be retooled and reprogrammed to think of strategy in the longer term, a distinct difference from Welch's approach.

Execute without Distraction

The secret to forward progress in difficult times is maintaining perspective, says Immelt. In sports, the ball does not always bounce your way. In business, the customer does not always show up for the close. You have done everything right to make the play or do the deal, but the laws of nature have another idea, injecting external forces that affect results. How leaders react to such adversity has everything to do with a company's fortunes years later.

Immelt has faced pressure on the job before, of course, and knows you cannot lose focus when things are not going your way. He remembers what it was like watching an entire business unit struggle under the weight of massive product recalls. He remembers fighting inflation and fixed contract prices at GE Plastics that doomed company quarterly profits.

From a personal standpoint, Immelt reduces stress and increases energy from rigors of the job by maintaining a life with limited areas of focus—"one company, one wife," he says. Outside of the office Immelt spends most of his free time, which he admits is not much, with his wife and college-aged daughter.

"I'm basically with my immediate family, or I'm at work," he says.

A self-professed proponent of "clean living," Immelt quit playin gpoker at night with friends years ago, just as he gave up golf junkets and vacations with extended family. Life is a marathon, he says, and in a job like his, mental agility is paramount in importance. So he's up early for exercise daily and drinks alcohol socially, but only in light moderation, saying "the last time I had too much to drink was probably 15 years ago." Immelt keeps his Blackberry on seven days a week because important news affecting a global company the size of GE never stops, but he balances that demand by giving up hobbies.

"I think you've got to lead a straightforward life, and I think it's important to have balance," says Immelt. "I love my company, I love my family, and I don't think I have to compromise between the two. I think I can do both. But it means you're going to have to make other tradeoffs."

Family helps Immelt maintain his perspective with the office, he says. They don't care about his job title or what company he works for, and they remind him to stick to qualities that have served him well along the way.

Immelt's personal strategy for overcoming tough times includes:

- Commit to learn every day (you need an incredible thirst for knowledge).
- Work hard with passion (competence and energy solve most problems).
- Give people a reason to trust (the world is more selective now, and trust is a differentiator).
- Have confidence (understand that you can make a difference).
- Be an optimist (the world has enough cynics today, and cynicism is corrosive; it creates excuses).

Ask Questions; Listen to the Answers

In the immediate months of turmoil after taking the job, Immelt's daily work plan was altered considerably. He had planned to travel the globe, meeting with employees, investors, and customers, and he expected to spend more time in the offices and on the factory floors of GE's many business operations around the world. Immelt has long been a believer of going to the source and seeing in person what is going on. This dates back to his days traveling with repairmen when he was in charge of customer service for the GE Appliance division. Now, he was seeing fewer company factories and spending more time in reassurance.

"When you take over a company like GE, you think you're going to visit 100 businesses. You're going to go see the factories you haven't seen before," said Immelt. "You're going to see a site in Texas and one in Canada and stuff like that."

Immelt's strategy initially was to keep his global travel and customer visits intact, even increasing them since he believed that the face of the company as reassurance was more important than ever before, but he doubled his time spent in investor and internal employee communications. The result was that Immelt spent almost 70 percent of his time those first two years traveling, investing in "touch" time with key people to say, hey, the eighth-largest company in the world (Enron) may have gone down, but we do not play in the same risky space that they did.

Working as a manager or executive at a multidimensional company like GE, one understands that mobility is necessity. Whether it involves time training at the leadership center in Crotonville, visiting a factory in Kentucky, or making a sales call to China, GE is spread operationally across more than 130 countries, and the company effectively has no true global headquarters, though offices in Fairfield, Connecticut, are officially listed as the company's primary domicile. For Immelt, this workplace demand comes easily. He's been on the road since his days in sales for GE Plastics in Dallas.

An avid reader who finishes on average one book a week, devouring such lengthy works as the 768-page *John Adams* by David McCullough or the book on Theodore Roosevelt, *River of Doubt*, by Candace Millard, Immelt spends his time on airplanes reading magazines and newspapers and studying history through books. Occasionally he reads novels, but Immelt leans toward nonfiction. He used to not read business books much, but more recently he has sought out more, particularly works on globalization and emerging markets like China where GE has significant vested interests. He frequently watches television programs like NBC's hit shows on the plane, opting for up-to-the-minute programs like CNBC when rigidly following his early morning exercise routine of being up at 5:30 a.m. and spending an hour or more on an elliptical machine. And he has a daily routine of periodicals.

"Every day I get through the (*Financial Times*)—I start with the FT—the *Wall Street Journal*, the *New York Times* business section, page six of the *New York Post*, but then I read *Modern Healthcare, Diagnostic Imaging, Modern Railroads, Entertainment Weekly* ..." said Immelt during an interview for the *Financial Times* in 2003, when the publication named him its man of the year.

Immelt is introspective and uses his quiet time on the road when not reading to meditate over what he's read or heard and learned in meetings and how it applies to GE's business model. He usually drives himself to work when he's spending time in his Fairfield office. Immelt lives just 20 minutes away, a short drive along tree-lined Connecticut state highway 15 in the picturesque bedroom community of New Canaan, which is composed of executive homes, quaint shops, and 20,000 residents. Immelt meditates during the commute about a variety of subjects, from meetings held during the day to the state of the world and the company.

When engaged with people, which is most of the time when he's not traveling, Immelt loves lively conversation and a quip and is not afraid to use an expletive in casual conversation in a nonoffensive manner. He rolls these words off his tongue with the harmless grace of a football player in the huddle talking with teammates as in, "Shit, I hate it when the stock price goes down."

But then he'll smile and laugh.

During interviews, he often asks questions himself, turning the interview into more of a conversation between two people rather than a grilling of one. But in customer and employee meetings he often does more listening than talking. The same can be said for his time at home, when he's there. With his wife, known affectionately as Andy, and his college-aged daughter, Immelt has independent eyes on the world away from the office and popular culture. When talking with customers and employees, he usually likes to know people's backgrounds and how they got their destination of the moment, and he asks often about experiences and insight, looking for cues he can plug into meetings and challenges faced later on.

When Immelt is asked a question, he typically gives what feels like a straight-shooting answer and is not afraid to say, as he did in one meeting, "I don't know." He once said his organizational behavior class was his least favorite in business school but he found out that in the world he spends most of his time with people. To know them and understand them, you have to listen to them.

"A 65-year-old in GE who still can learn is vital to me," says Immelt. "A 30-year-old who thinks they know it all has no value to me."

While listening to customers and employees during his global travels in the turbulent times of his first two years on the job as chairman and CEO, Immelt says he found his own reassurances. He was reminded that, while external influences he and the company could not control had so drastically changed, the core strengths of GE were firmly intact. Instead of spending too much time trying to put out the fires, they needed to build firewalls and trenches for insulation and strength. He wishes he would have moved faster in the wake of 9/11 and Enron to refocus on the company's foundation, ignoring outside attacks like the one by Bill Gross that he could not control, but he knows that at the time, it was important to hear and properly assess.

What he learned about the company matched perfectly with the ambition he had in taking the job in the first place—that GE needed a revolution in the twenty-first century to not only survive but thrive in the changing world economy.

GE was already global, but Immelt says that the company needed to push hard beyond its boundaries to write a new definition of what it means to be a global corporation. GE already had long-term strategy as an initiative, yet Immelt felt that the company needed to invest more resources in the endeavor. And, while GE has been known for its innovation dating back to Edison's discoveries, Immelt believed that the company needed to internally create more growth opportunities.

CHAPTER 6

CULTIVATE BIG IDEAS

"... if we can spur our growth rate without losing our productivity edge, GE will keep being the most admired company into the next century."

—JEFF IMMELT

Long-term leadership is about the effective layering of strengths.

The premise according to Jeff Immelt is to remove weaknesses, building upon core strengths with new ones, one on top of another. Take GE's leadership center at Crotonville for instance. Before Jack Welch became CEO, the center had been serving employees for more than two decades, but Welch took it to the next level, making Crotonville in a span of two decades synonymous internally with the company's drive to be the best.

After Welch retired, Immelt continued the legacy of leadership training at Crotonville. By his seventh year on the job, he was pouring more than $1 billion into corporate training and professional development, a figure believed unequaled by any corporation in the world. Think about it. Most CEOs would love to have a billion bucks to spend after expenses, but GE puts that amount as an expense into employee continuing education.

Even in the hardest times, like recessionary periods in 2002 and 2008, Immelt says GE never backed off training investment in its 300,000-plus employees, the ones charged with powering the company's growth into the future, to salvage the bottom line. He understands that GE can call a halt to most of the company's training spending at any time, thereby improving short-term numbers. The concept could be tempting in tough economic conditions, but Immelt believes that sustainability for GE is about maintaining its management culture. That is done by training employees in a patented cross-company and cross-functional way that has been good for GE over the decades.

A company acquiring new businesses by the dozen like GE typically benefits on an annual basis from sending employees through such structured training because it keeps them attached to the same reinforcing nerve center. That's why GE's top 189 executives have been on average in the past decade to at least 12 months of leadership training at the Crotonville center. Immelt supported the training legacy established by Welch from day one on the job, and he has continued this support at the highest reasonable level, even at the lofty cost of $1 billion annually.

"We're in a recession now," said Immelt in late 2008, "and we're spending as much on training as we did in a flush economy. Most everywhere else today, the amount spent on leadership training is going down. But I spend 30 percent of my time (as CEO) on human resources, and we continue to invest because the software of this company is very valuable.

"We have always believed that building strong leaders is a strategic imperative," Immelt says. "When times are easy, leadership can be taken for granted. When the world is turbulent, you appreciate great people."

Shortly after taking over as GE's chairman and CEO, Immelt concluded from his touch and meditation moments in the field that in-depth employee training was not enough for the company to continue its reign as a blue-chip corporate growth engine into its next century of business. Having well-trained employees means little if you don't push them and also allow them to unleash talent and creativity, sparking innovation and growth from within for the longer term.

"For me to say that I wasn't at all caring about quarterly earnings and things like that, my nose would grow," says Immelt. "You've got to be able to do both (short-term and long-term objectives), but at the same time I run a company that has been around for 130 years, and so a lot of what we do has to be about the future."

When Jack Welch took over General Electric as CEO in 1981, company revenues were just $25 billion so the company's future was right before him. He came along in a recessionary period, had money to acquire businesses, and the acumen to cut costs once he had businesses in hand. Focusing on the consumer in North America and in Europe, Welch was able in his tenure to apply strong management principles to robust economic expansion occurring on the two continents over two decades to achieve massive growth.

But by the time Welch turned the company reins over to Jeff Immelt in 2001, GE's annual revenues were well over $100 billion and the economy was at the end of a bullish cycle.

Then, as the world quickly changed after the turn of the century, Immelt found himself leading a company facing significant challenges in longer-term growth.

Picking the proverbial low-hanging fruit can be quite productive until it is gone. If a big company like GE is going to continue to reward shareholders and employees as a growth company, ingenuity must be invoked or else a company known for decades as innovative becomes stagnant and old-school. Growing a giant is not easy, even when the giant is known to be a relatively nimble multibusiness one like GE.

Acquisitions can certainly deliver growth opportunities. But for GE to make a buy, a company must be for sale because internal management policy strongly adhered to by Immelt has long been that hostile takeovers are out of the question. So even though GE typically has billions in available cash and financing to make strategic buys, moves are not made unless the following criteria are met:

1. The company is for sale.
2. The primary product or products hold significant potential for longer-term growth.
3. The profile fits with GE's business portfolio and management and service capabilities.
4. The price is right.

Even though no company in the world likely makes more acquisitions annually on average than GE, far more potential buys are considered that are turned down because either the fit or the price is not right. More often the deciding factor is price since GE usually knows at the outset which businesses meld with its mix. And one Immelt characteristic which may come as somewhat of a surprise to someone making assumptions from a distance is his tendency when considering acquisitions to be more of a bargain hunter than a premium payer.

Immelt is one of the best paid executives in the world—he earned more than $9 million in salary and bonuses in 2007 not including exercised stock options and he lives in a tony suburban Connecticut neighborhood. He also has a second home, an apartment at Manhattan's ritzy One Beacon Court on the Upper East Side, along with building neighbors Jack Welch and NBC news anchor Brian Williams. But when it comes to spending company money, he will not write a big check in acquisition just because he can, using instead GE's deep accounting department to scale value.

He will pay fairly, but rarely at a premium without good reason. Examples abound, but one goes back to his earliest days in office when NBC flirted with buying a National Basketball Association broadcast package. He loves sports and wanted the network to consider expanding its offerings, but he felt the price tag was too high and walked away. Another example is when he refused in 2005 to pay top dollar to purchase the live-action film studio of DreamWorks SKG, which ultimately sold to Viacom for $1.6 billion. Many of NBC's top executives did not agree with the decision, but Immelt did not feel the valuation was fair, so he walked away, allowing another company to make the deal even though GE could have easily written the check.

Immelt is certainly no acquisitions bottom fisher, considering that GE typically acquires only businesses that are among the best in a particular field. He believes, however, that GE is the world leader at scaling businesses and does not ever want the company's spending ability to impair its reasonability.

"I was watching one of the news shows (recently), and they were talking about subprime," Immelt says, "and this guy was making the case that ... guys like me don't track the details—that's why Citigroup failed or Merrill Lynch failed versus private equity and these guys are combing through the details. That's bs. We comb through details. We have processes that allow us to comb through details."

"Believe me," says Immelt, "there's not one point in time that any of us ever run GE like a big company. We run it like it was a grocery store on the corner. We look at details, we look at processes, and we look at people like it was not some obscure big company. So we may run into it some day, but we've been able to scale the culture and the values and the people in a way that I don't think we're close to that level yet.

"We plant seeds. We don't have to be right all the time, but the good part of GE is that we know how to scale businesses."

Often, GE does strike in acquisition consideration when everything aligns, like in 2008 when the company successfully bid through its entertainment subsidiary NBC Universal for the specialized Internet and broadcast company The Weather Channel. Joining with private equity firms Blackstone Group and Bain Capital, GE orchestrated a deal for roughly $3.5 billion in an effort to strengthen its media presence with one of the strongest niche brands on both cable television and the World Wide Web.

With weather-watching in the United States increasingly becoming both necessity and hobby as unpredictability and catastrophic events like hurricanes and blizzards significantly affect lives and economics, the NBCU management team saw significant long-term growth potential and brand leverage. Immelt watched the proceedings closely from the sidelines but was not intricately involved in the division's large purchase. Instead, he allowed his team to structure the deal, and he was ready to step in with approval or veto depending on the price and anticipated returns.

He approved the deal, confirming that he firmly believes owning NBC is in the best interests of the company and shareholders despite repeated external cries for GE to sell its media assets dating back to the Welch days. No, Immelt effectively said in allowing the deal, not only are we not going to sell NBC Universal, but we are going to strengthen the entertainment division by expanding it with a complementary branded property that owns its space—weather journalism.

Invest in Tomorrow

Foraging for the future does not often come so easily though as that natural acquisition nugget did for NBCU. Therefore, Immelt firmly believes that neither GE's respected management skills nor the company's ability to make acquisitions is enough to lead the company throughout its next century of business. With an established global management network and more than $180 billion in annual sales, GE has the girth needed to hire and keep talented personnel to manage its businesses. The company can usually service customers and manage the bottom line in the right environment but without the best, most innovative products, GE has less in the way of firm footing to stand on. Without something extraordinary to sell, the company's advantages quickly disappear.

"The thing is you can be Six Sigma," Immelt said. "You can do great delivery. You can be great in China. You can do everything else well, but if you don't have a good product, you are not going to sell much."

GE's solution, according to Immelt: "We fund product leadership."

Inside the company, the operative words during Immelt's tenure with respect to funding product leadership are "imagination breakthroughs."

The concept emanates from Immelt's initiative of organic growth, the concept of business expansion relating to increased output and sales from within without relying upon mergers and acquisitions. Immelt's strategy is that GE will grow from within through internally generated means at two to three times the world gross domestic product (GDP). The initiative harkens back to naysayers like Bill Gross suggesting the company could only buy its way to growth.

When Immelt first announced the organic growth plan in 2004, more than a few skeptics outside the company raised doubting eyebrows. For a corporation the size of GE to grow from within at a rate which amounts to 8 percent or more per year seemed like a stretch, if not an impossibility. Almost no company could expect to achieve such a lofty goal, much less one the size of GE. But not so surprisingly, perhaps, Immelt and the company have overdelivered in almost every quarter since the organic growth initiative was announced, pushing toward 8 or 9 percent. This is achieved through obvious means such as expanding good services into areas around the world like China and India where they are in more demand, but the backbone of the premise goes straight back to GE's pioneering days and innovation leadership tradition.

In the beginning, there were scientists like Thomas Edison, who developed the incandescent electric lamp and founded the Edison General Electric Company which would ultimately morph into today's GE; William Coolidge, who helped perfect the company's light by inventing the ductile tungsten filament which made its incandescent lamps decidedly longer-lasting and durable and contributed significantly to development of both the tube and portable X-ray machine; and Charles Steinmetz, a scientist who convinced company leaders in 1900 to invest in a research laboratory to find new means of growth.

Nevermind that GE was just an eight-year-old company at the turn of the nineteenth century and that no other company in the United States operated an independent research and development laboratory. GE opened a center to foster corporate innovation in a carriage barn in Steinmetz's back yard. More than a century later, Immelt's commitment to fostering GE's imagination breakthroughs and organic growth may not seem like such a stretch. After all, the GE Global Research Center has long been a private sector leader in ingenuity, contributing literally thousands of patents over the years in fields ranging from health care to aviation to industrial lighting.

By the 1980s, however, mild complacency had set in at GE's research center, likely resulting from the leadership-oriented emphasis on Crotonville. The tone at the research center was almost more academic than business in nature. Naturally, this did not match well with the hard-charging, bottom-line style of the CEO, Welch, who went on to change the center's operational structure. Rather than simply funding the center from GE's general budget, Welch funded it directly from each of the company's operating divisions—numbering 13 at the time. The strategy forced the center and its scientists to earn budget through results, enveloping research in a produce-or-else environment. For the research center, the move was needed and effectively linked corporate demands with innovation. The full impact of transformation did not take effect, however, until Immelt took office, emphatically shifting the company's strategy toward innovation cultivation, or imagination breakthroughs.

Predictably, Jack Welch had little patience with investigative science inside the corporation. For the most part, the company's future was now and that ran through Crotonville, Six Sigma, and GE's array of management processes and demands. The research center rarely grabbed Welch's attention unless something promised to deliver hundreds of millions of dollars or more in profits quickly. Welch bet heavily on the very successful GE90 aircraft engine which revolutionized aviation, for example, but he quickly lost interest in findings that were vague and without a clear, immediate, and obvious path to profitability.

Welch wanted to get big fast, so he initiated the strategy at GE of growing through acquisition. Before he became CEO, the company had traditionally clung to a belief that it was better to manage your own businesses without taking on others. But in 1985, Welch orchestrated GE's purchase of the communications company RCA, which included the NBC Television Network, said to be his first major countercultural step at the company. With RCA's business, GE zoomed to seventh on the Fortune 500 list, and Welch figured out that he was onto something good. The acquisitions strategy under Welch continued throughout his tenure until his last big attempt, buying Honeywell, failed to materialize.

Enter Immelt, who is far more salesman than scientist by training and experience. While peddling products in the field, he learned that even the best salesperson is nothing without the latest, greatest, best products to offer. So from the first day Immelt became GE's chairman and CEO, he had a plan to continue Welch's acquisition strategy while restoring the innovative, grow-from-within culture.

"Jeff has a real appreciation for the value of great technology and how much easier it is to sell when you've got it and how much harder it is to sell when you don't," says John Rice, GE vice chairman and president and CEO of GE's Technology Infrastructure division.

The process of stepping up support of internal innovation was twofold. First, Immelt invested $100 million in upgrading the GE Global Research Center in Niskayuna, New York, which looked, according to Immelt, like "his old high school." In the renovation, GE built an on-site lodge for visitors and expanded conference and research facilities which were dated and unable to serve large company gatherings. The idea behind expanding the lodge was to create another company nerve center in addition to Crotonville. If the leadership center fostered management for the entire company, the research center should foster innovation for the entire company.

Immelt also funded global research expansion, boosting centers around the world in places like Shanghai, China; Bangalore, India; and Munich, Germany. He put a seasoned company business executive in charge who values technology but also understands the intricacies of a balance sheet and profit and loss statement. Then he placed on management a burden of innovation equal to the burden inside the company which has long existed on making quarterly and annual profit targets. Ideas cannot merely be a bonus from management. Ideas have to be demanded from management.

"At the Global Research Center, we can be an aggregator," says Immelt.

Simply, Immelt believed that for GE to deliver in 2010 and in 2020 the way it did in 1990 and 2000, something had to change. Short-term sighting alone was not going to be enough. GE needed to blend the eye to the future held by the likes of Edison and Steinmetz with the delivery demands of Welch to take a step forward under Immelt with the stronger research layer added on top of the existing management layer. As a result, his imagination breakthroughs program forces leadership to deliver three idea proposals each year which will be reviewed by the Immelt-led commercial council, the most recently established annual high-ranking employee gathering which fosters innovation internally. The idea proposal presented by managers to the commercial council must be able to generate $100 million in revenue growth and open new doors either geographically, in different business categories, or with new customers.

"One of the things Jeff talks about a lot are imagination breakthroughs," says John Rice, a company director and head of an infrastructure division. "That is code for a process he developed which helps cultivate ideas not quite yet ready for prime time. It gives them room to breathe, air cover for investment, and a chance to succeed, whereas in the normal process, they might not.

"There have been dozens—hundreds—since we introduced the concept," says Rice. "It helps a company like ours learn to grow organically. It creates a culture where people are passionate about their ideas for growth. They have space and time to develop the ideas, and we listen to them. We don't always say yes, but we love them."

Immelt participates in the imagination breakthroughs directly, with half a dozen or more reaching his desk each month since the program began. He reviews the ideas with program managers sitting at the table, ready to answer questions. He does not want some long-winded PowerPoint presentations or bold predictions of what it can be. Rather, Immelt looks over a short idea outline accompanied by an actual picture of what the idea might be, from a revolutionary imaging machine to a water desalination plant, and asks a few questions, among which these three typically lead the list:

1. What is the biggest internal barrier you face?
2. What is the biggest external barrier you face?
3. What is the revenue flow?

Everybody Plays

Welch, of course, was famous for how he ran GE's Session C meetings, human resources affairs during which he critiqued the company's top several hundred managers himself, often in the most demanding ways, almost always relating specifically to quarterly results performances. GE's Session C meetings were instituted years before Welch arrived, but he moved them away from the company's Fairfield offices, making them day-long events at each of GE's respective businesses. There, Welch and his human resources team went over the specific job performance of each manager in painstaking detail.

In the evening, Welch had dinner with them in a social setting, looking for behavioral cues. In these meetings Welch liked to rate GE's management team into three groups based on numbers performances and values that matched the company's goals and standards. Welch thereby identified the top 20 percent of performers for promotion; the middle 70 percent of performers as needing help; and the bottom 10 percent as needing help finding other professional opportunities.

The strategy was well-documented in case studies and established as corporate lore, helping to shape Welch's aura as a unique twentieth-century business leader. But GE insiders say that the human resources process was sometimes misunderstood by outsiders. Says Rice: "There was a point in time where I think people thought the bottom 10 were blindfolded and taken out to the back parking lot and executed at sunset. That never happened.

"What typically happened is one-third of the bottom 10 took the feedback and made it out as is; one-third were probably in the wrong jobs, great individual contributors put in a manager's job who needed to go back; and one-third who recognized GE was not the best place for them and left.

"But what it forced and what exists today is a level of candor," says Rice.

Immelt and GE still conduct the Session C meetings, but the process has evolved somewhat. Talk in review sessions focuses on "candid, straightforward feedback so everybody knows where they stand" and no longer specifically breaks the group into mandatory percentage categories.

Everyone, says Immelt, has a next level of performance, including the chairman and CEO, the vice chairmen, and the top-performing managers. Whether you are the all-star slugger or you are still not getting on base often enough, there is something more everyone can do. The bottom line is that you want an environment where leaders have an obligation to sit down with the people who are not measuring up and tell them where they are not measuring up, what they need to do to improve, and make sure that if there is not improvement that there has to be another answer.

Don't think for a moment, though, that succeeding as a manager at GE got any easier under Immelt. To the contrary, many say. Though his guidelines and style differ from those of the past, the demands, in many ways, can be harder because the environment is so decidedly different. Making quarterly numbers can be harder, and managers are also pushed to contribute big ideas on a regular basis. In other words, quarterly results are expected, but top managers must also contribute to the company's long-term viability with new business concepts.

"Nobody is allowed not to play," said Immelt. "Nobody can say, 'I'm going to sit this one out.' That's the way you drive change."

Call it a road map to success for the twenty-first century. To be an effective manager after the new millennium, you have to perform for the short term, the medium term, and the longer term. A great company operating in a difficult environment cannot starve its future through cost-cutting and low reinvestment, both in ideas and capital.

"We set a goal in organic growth just because I thought that was an important metric in terms of how to build a growth culture inside the company," Immelt says. "And organic growth is really a function of getting in the right markets and then having initiatives that are going to allow you to grow organically over a long period of time. And I'd like that to be the major thrust of what we do, is organic growth. I just think it's the most investor friendly."

To make sure GE managers deliver ideas for organic growth, Immelt put in place a colors-based grading scale for growth contribution similar to the numbers performance scale used by Welch. A red rating means that a manager needs improvement; those with yellow ratings are faring satisfactorily; while those with green ratings are strong in the growth department.

As a result, many who work under Immelt say he is not as difficult as Welch was in a face-to-face meeting or while being talked to before a group but that in the longer term he can be harder to work for because his expectations are more varied. Under Immelt, quarterly results and values remain important, but leaders also have meetings with the commercial council where they are expected to deliver big, business-changing ideas.

"Organic growth is the driver," said Immelt. "Acquisitions are secondary to that—I can't see us go out and pay a start-up $100 million for technology that, if we had just spent $2 million a year for 10 years, we could've done a better job at."

Immelt is hardly a shrinking violet type among employees even though he is quite approachable, and underlings refer to him by his first name—Jeff. Like Welch, he is demanding, but he is demanding in a different sort of way. Making quarterly numbers, he said, is an expectation. He does not have to rate management on making numbers since all are expected to deliver. Those who don't may have a good reason. Maybe the company is operating in the wrong space. Or the market is softening and the manager did a good job just keeping it afloat. If the manager is underperforming, he's quick to make a change, he says. But it is more than short-term numbers in the tougher, turn-of-the-century business environment.

"Naysayers," says Immelt, "think our organic growth goal is too big, that it is against our company's culture. They say we can only buy our growth. But I felt we needed to achieve a balance. We tried to set a goal and felt we know how to achieve it. I knew if we could use our scale, we could reach a higher goal, and that's what we have done."

For GE to thrive and deliver returns in the future as it has in the past—"another decade of 4 percent growth," he once told top company managers, "and GE will cease to be a great company"—requires managers delivering results in the short term, medium term, *and* long term.

"We're now in a slow-growth world," said Immelt. "Things were different 25 years ago." Oil was under $30 a barrel; most growth came from the developed world; we were a country at peace. After I came in as CEO, I looked at the world post-9/11 and realized that over the next 10 or 20 years, there just was not going to be much tailwind. It would be a more global market, it would be more driven by innovation, and a premium would be placed on companies that could generate their own growth.

"We have to change the company—to become more innovation driven—in order to deal with this new environment," says Immelt. "It's the right thing for investors. Productivity is still very important, but if you look back at GE's businesses over the past decade or so, those that have been managed for both productivity and growth have done the best."

The idea is to make management personally responsible for innovation; Immelt and GE must cultivate innovation leaders. They cannot assume that the big acquisition is just around the corner nor can they expect divisions like finance to produce the kinds of results delivered in the 1990s. Besides, for decades GE has used its top-pay and stringent hiring requirements to hire as well as almost any company in the world.

Bright minds, supported by other bright minds as well as tools like imbedded management processes designed to foster ideas, should be able to bring creative solutions to world challenges to the commercial council table. Just as GE leaders and managers have long been held to quarterly performance standards, GE leaders and managers are now held to annual idea standards. For Immelt and GE, the move essentially distributes risk responsibility more widely in hopes of getting more corporate return for the internal idea bets placed.

"Achieving this kind of growth depends on making it the personal mission of everyone here," says Immelt. "If we want, we can cloak ourselves in the myth of the professional manager and hide any problem in the process flowchart. But if I want people to take more risks, solve bigger problems, and grow the business in a way that's never been done before, I have to make it personal."

INVEST IN INNOVATION

"If you want to be in the front seat of history, come to work at my company."

—JEFF IMMELT

Mark Little talks about GEs commitment to fostering innovation and breakthroughs the company has made and is making with the ease of a veteran backed by experience who has not lost his passion for the job. Little has been a company employee since 1978 and the ninth person to serve as director of the GE Global Research Center since its founding in 1900, yet in his three decades as a GE employee Little has spent more time solving numbers, people, and product problems than he has birthing big ideas. As a manager and executive he ran GE components ranging from gas turbines to power generation, and he has served as business development leader for GE Energy, one of the company's largest divisions.

But Little's knowledge of engineering and understanding of how promising technology comes to market combined with his business experience was reason enough for Immelt to make him GE's chief technology officer, charging him with shepherding innovation. Already a company director, Little was named by Immelt to remake the GE Global Research Center into a corporate nerve center in much the same way as the leadership center in Crotonville serves the company.

At businesses of all sizes, cross-company and cross-functional teamwork is beneficial. At multidimensional GE, where leverage from one department or division to another is an operative buzzword, both are necessities. The cross-fertilization and cross-pollination that results from creating research and technology teams including GE employees from multiple disciplines to work on the same project allows the company to draw upon multiple strengths while also plugging in breakthroughs to many different, seemingly unrelated businesses that might otherwise have no connection.

Take the lotus leaf as one example. Spend some time in the hallways of the GE research labs which sit inconspicuously along the picturesque Mohawk River in Niskayuna, New York, and find out quickly that a small group of the company's 30,000 technologists—most work in specialized divisions, like aviation, energy, or health care; roughly 10 percent work independently for the corporation at the Global Research Center—are over the top about the lotus leaf, or what they learned from the lotus leaf. The discovery hullaballoo started when the company's materials technologists working in nanotechnology—the control of matter on an atomic or molecular scale—began trying to emulate a lotus leaf, which repels water and does a sort of self-cleaning in the process.

Place a droplet of water on the lotus leaf and watch it bead into a perfect sphere which easily rolls off, taking particles along for the ride. Just the kind of observation that gets Jeff Immelt excited, eliciting corporate funding above and beyond GE's divisional research investment. If GE researchers can develop material to emulate the lotus leaf, imagine the applications, Little says. Airplane wings and engines tend to take on ice, but maybe not if made of material that repelled like the lotus leaf.

By bringing in leaders from different companies and organizations to see technologies, GE obtains multiple benefits. A finding originally investigated in one area can be parlayed into another. Examples at the research center are abundant. For instance, when GE looked into the security business, researchers adapted technology from the health-care imaging division for use in scanning baggage.

Among the ways GE fosters cross-company and cross-discipline teamwork now under Immelt (whereas before not as much was done under Welch) is through contact with a vast global business network during what's called the Session T sessions held at the Global Research Center. The T, naturally, stands for technology, so in these sessions held three times per year, the research center brings in a marketing team from one business and a technology team from an altogether different business to meet with scientists.

"They talk about a marketplace need, translate that into a technical need, and then brainstorm around that," says the 52-year-old Little.

For instance, emissions requirements for railroad locomotives are getting tougher, according to Little. Most companies might not care, but GE does because its transportation unit is the world's leading manufacturer of diesel-electric locomotives. So GE has studied such new technology concepts as combustion control, catalytic systems, and hybrid locomotives.

Some people might find such talk droll, but GE has a knack for parlaying technologies across its business grid, and the Session T is the type of pollinating program that does the work.

Little says that another example is how the company expanded use of material from its patented GE90 aircraft-engine fan blade. Measuring 4 feet long and weighing less than 50 pounds, the blade is one of a kind. At GE, through its central-focused research center the company can ask where else the material can be used. Through Session T meetings, the energy business learned about the lightweight material, seeking to apply it to wind turbine blades measuring 150 feet long.

"The cross-business fertilization of research was marginal under Jack Welch, but Jeff has created an excitement and energy around the concept," said Noel M. Tichy, a University of Michigan professor who used to lead GE's leadership center at Crotonville.

No company in the world, of course, works with as many moving parts as GE so the benefits can be many. From wind turbines to small engines, the company can find dozens of profitable uses for a water repellant, self-cleaning industrial coating. So Immelt and GE stepped up on the lotus leaf–inspired findings, investing millions in the project even though shareholders would not see benefits for perhaps as much as five years.

"Jeff puts a premium on risk taking, thinking about investing in new ventures, small businesses that can become big businesses, and not pulling the plug too quickly on good ideas," says John Rice. "Maybe we stumble out of the starting blocks, but it is the right vision and the right strategy, and given a year or two we will get it right."

GE nanotechnologists effectively came up with a way—their term for it is superhydrophobicity—to make a common polymer repel fluids. When a 20-year company employee shows the patented process in action, first through a small demonstration in a petri dish, then on a simulated aircraft engine in a manufactured frigid wind tunnel, she acts as if she can hardly hide her passion, even though the visitor knows she's shown the same experiments dozens of times, if not more. So far, she points out during the larger experiment, GE's patented metals coating is getting 60 to 70 percent reduction in ice accumulation on the aircraft engine. She imagines out loud different repellant results the same material might have on cars, eliminating bug adhesion, and on GE's wind turbines, eliminating collections including water, bugs, dirt, and ice.

By working from the research center as a central point with GE's different divisions, she says, the company can leverage its technology advancement into multiple breakthroughs like that, from aviation to energy. Similar stories unfold up and down the hallways since GE's research center is widely considered one of the few best corporate types in the world. Stop along the hallway, for instance, to visit with a company research biologist—literally dozens of biologists have been hired at GE's research center since Immelt took charge, initiating biotechnology research—and hear about how GE plans to change the way physicians will potentially be able to diagnose and treat cancer in the future.

The company's new fluorescent image guidance system, in development for the three years since Immelt committed to upgrading GE's research facility and staff, is about to be delivered to GE's Medical Diagnostics division where it will undergo clinical trials. Employees will have fingers crossed about the innovative machine which promises to better differentiate for physicians cancerous and healthy cells. But in business, it's a big bet, not unlike what large drug companies face trying to bring a new product to market.

GE's research biologists and fellow project team members face a similar challenge trying to change the way the global pathology field works assessing and storing patient data. The general concept of this GE research project, conducted in the same building with crossover from some of the same team members, is to improve patient diagnosis through digital applications. Slide storage in many large hospitals takes up rooms, and retrieving a patient's slide can be a chore. By developing processes to scan slides, digitizing them for viewing on a computer screen, pathologists can have a higher diagnosis success rate and easier access to patient files.

When a visitor suggests that the manual method pathologists use to study patient data—slides under a microscope—is already effective and perhaps more time efficient than weaving through digital files, the biologist has a quick response. Improved diagnosis, she admits, will not be readily adapted industrywide if GE cannot make the process fast and efficient. However, by working closely with a chosen educational healthcare leader—the University of Pittsburgh Medical Center— GE is trying to bridge the gap between corporate hopes and marketplace needs.

Immelt, GE Healthcare, and the research team know that the technology is leading edge, just as they know that the diagnostic imaging machine is leading edge, but bringing promising new models to business is never easy, even for a company the size of GE. Patience, then, becomes necessary for the CEO who wants to truly deliver organic growth opportunities which hold potential for being tomorrow's bottom-line drivers.

"I respect Jack Welch immensely," says Little, speaking from his office at the GE Global Research Center. "Jack has a Ph.D. in chemical engineering. Jeff has a Harvard MBA. Jack fully understood how important technology was, but he was deeply cynical about technology going off doing something that was not relevant (to the bottom line).

"Jeff talks about technology much more directly," says Little. "Jeff says managers who cut technology funding when they are just trying to make quarterly numbers are weak managers. [Cutting technology funding] is not viewed by Jeff as a sign of a strong GE manager."

Patience Is Indeed a Virtue

After a long day at the GE's Niskayuna research center, the idea is to catch a quiet, relaxing dinner with time to ponder absorbed information. Plans do not always work out that way though since a nearby Italian restaurant selected for dinner, Schenectady's Cella Bistro, is filled on a Tuesday night mostly with GE employees and their guests. Overheard conversations might be titillating, for a research zealot. For instance, one gentleman waiting for a table shares with peers how he has been assigned a project extracting algae from water and finding a way to turn the process into energy. Another gentleman discusses looking into hydrogen as automotive food before being jokingly reprimanded.

"We don't want to be in the fuel business," he is told.

Seemingly only the waitress knows nothing of GE. So when she comes in to take an order, the customer decides to find out what if anything she knows about GE in a moment that went something like this:

"I'll have the herring and dill sour cream from the tapas menu."

"Anything else?" the waitress asks.

"What do you know about GE?"

"Well," she says, "our co-owner is a chemist at GE research. He's in the kitchen now. I'll ask him."

"He's in the kitchen now?"

The clock is well past seven in the evening. She explains that Dr. James Cella who owns the restaurant with his son, loves cooking and serving food as a hobby. His son is the executive chef and sometimes after a long day at the office Dr. Cella drops by the restaurant in the evening to lend a helping hand. This makes for an 80-hour work week, but apparently does nothing to diminish productivity at the office since Dr. Cella can be found listed on a board hanging in the research center lobby which names him as being among company leaders in patents obtained for GE—he is responsible for more than 50 patents.

"Yes," says the waitress. "It's true. He loves it."

One does not know if she means the kitchen or the laboratory, but either is acceptable.

"Ask him then what he thinks about Jeff Immelt."

She pauses momentarily.

The New York Yankees baseball team is playing against their rival, the Boston Red Sox, on television. The waitress is a Boston Red Sox fan, even though she lives in New York and dates a Yankee fan. But she watches every inning of Yankees games she can when the Red Sox are not on the tube, revealing a typical love-hate sports relationship with the New York team.

In the televised game, the Red Sox are batting. A slow ground ball is hit in the infield, passing the pitcher and ambling between the shortstop and third baseman. The pitcher turns and watches the ball pass. Rodriguez, the Yankees' all-star fielder, closes in. He reaches down with his right hand, trying to clasp the moving ball with a bare hand. But his thumb closes before he has fielded the ball cleanly, and it is bobbled for a rare error, allowing the batter to reach first safely.

The waitress can hardly contain her enthusiasm, charging toward the kitchen to chide her boss, the world-leading chemist who is juggling the myriad orders before him. Dr. Cella is a Yankees fan, of course, and she enthusiastically tells him first about the Rodriguez error. Then, she asks an oh-by-the-way question on behalf of the paying customer.

"So what do you think about Jeff Immelt? This guy out there wants to know."

The conveyed response is firm. Just reporting what the boss said, she says.

"Jeff Immelt," she says, "is more patient (than Jack Welch). He is willing to wait for a good thing to develop. [Shareholders] may not always understand, but [Immelt] is looking for the breakthrough. They will be rewarded [with his patience]."

The point for Immelt and GE is not to throw money at promising discoveries without regard for the short-term bottom line or results. But they want to restore GE's position as a world leader in patents. For most of the twentieth century, even until 1986, GE had more patents than any other corporation, but by the time Welch retired in 2001 GE was no longer even in the top 20 ranking of companies holding patents.

If anything, Little says the pressure for research to be handed over to company divisions so it can find its way into the revenue-producing pipeline is as real today, if not more so, than before. And Immelt keeps a close watch on research developments, particularly in regard to progress. In fact in early August of 2008, just before Immelt was taking off for summer vacation, he asked Little for an update on all projects underway at GE's Global Research Center with updated time-lines. Little mapped out a color-coded chart with red, yellow, and green, with green noting projects that are on track, yellow noting projects that need improvements, and red noting projects that are behind schedule and facing challenges.

Not exactly beach reading for most people, but the score-card system of progress is a simple and effective way for Immelt to stay in the loop with the center and Little without waiting for formal meetings and presentations.

"Jeff is constantly pushing us to examine our investments in R&D to make sure we have enough," says John Rice. "That does not mean it is a blank check and no consequences, but he treats it as a significant priority."

Create Healthy Tension

For research and development and other initiatives that do not contribute directly to quarterly company results, a system must be in place that creates a natural pressure point conveying to employees daily that advancements in science and technology are expected to deliver revenue growth in as timely a manner as possible. The longer the development phase, the bigger the payoff should be. And promises made, as in, "We'll have that ready to hand off within six months," should be promises kept.

Immelt upgraded the center with a wave of the corporate wand through $100 million in infrastructure investment and more investment in personnel, adding disciplines like biotechnology which did not previously exist. But each project must struggle with the processes and demands of profitable business to gain and retain funding.

One way Immelt works to ensure both research productivity and return on investment is a combination funding formula which includes his direct involvement. The tension created dates back to the Welch era when project funding came directly from company divisions. This creates a beneficial pull-pull profit mentality, but that alone is not enough, according to Immelt. Some projects may hold promise, but they might be a riskier bet, and they may not be quite ready for a prime time budget. So Immelt works closely with Little to identify areas needing corporate funding which he controls. The result is a GE Global Research Center budget in excess of $500 million annually which works out like this:

- 60 percent of the funding comes from GE businesses. The businesses get to decide how that money is used, maintaining constant information exchange with research team members. Typically businesses teams assessing progress and providing development input are cross-functional, including management, technologists, and sales and marketing personnel. If at any time they feel that dollars are not being well spent, they can pull the plug.

- Another 27 percent comes from GE corporate—Jeff Immelt. GE's chairman and CEO, effectively tells Mark Little and team something like, "You guys are the experts. This is a risky bet, but it might pay off big, so here is some money. Go figure it out and keep me apprised."
- Another 13 percent comes from the many outside partnerships GE has ranging from government, educational, and nonprofit entities.

Outside of the Global Research Center, each company division has billions in funds which can be allocated to research and development, and Immelt keeps close tabs on those dollars as well. His primary formal forum to discuss research ideas is during the annual commercial council meetings he established as the foundation of funding. There, Little sits along with Immelt and his executive team members, and they listen to pitches of literally dozens of the so-called big ideas generated which are vying to become corporate imagination breakthroughs. No money is allocated unless real promise is shown that work can one day positively affect GE's bottom line. The experienced technologists understand, of course, that they can best serve the company with a pipeline mentality: Get the oil flowing; then keep it coming in a steady stream.

Keys to fostering innovation, according to Immelt include:

- Prepare the organization to innovate.
- Pick the right places to innovate.
- Make innovation pay for innovation.

Immelt says that his decision to invest so heavily in the research from both an infrastructure perspective and an ongoing investment strategy with direct involvement from the chairman's office came about for three reasons.

"First, 25 years ago … Welch looked at Crotonville, the leadership institute," Immelt said. "The place looked like crap. He put money into it and said, 'We're going to make this a showcase for GE.' In a multibusiness company, for building culture, you need things like that. Flash forward. [Second] our Global Research Center in Schenectady looked lousy. The physical plant, the amount of customers who came through every year—we'd just fallen behind. It's one of our best assets. So the first thing we did is just fix that physical plant to give it the look of a winner. Then we globalized it and opened up centers in Bangalore and Shanghai and Munich.

"Third, we had a high-priced job shop," Immelt said. "We had more than 2,000 projects being done in that infrastructure. I cut it to 80. I went and said, 'Molecular medicine—we're going to own it. Nanotechnology—we're going to own it. Renewable energy, energy efficiency, environmental technology—we're going to own it. All this (stuff) around some guy saying, I'm selling billable hours in the research center, I say throw that all out. You all work for me. I'm going to tell you exactly what I want you to do, and here's what the business is going to pay for. It's going to be very clear. Here's what you have to deliver on.'"

For GE's Global Research Center, the process seems to be working. Funding has increased every year since Immelt has been in charge, despite some large company divisions like plastics being sold. All pieces of the pie, from the businesses, from corporate, and from external partners, have been getting larger with the increased emphasis on research.

"I run a company that has been around for 130 years, and so a lot of what we do has to be about the future," Immelt says. "... I protect $6 billion of funding in research and development. And I have line of sight to it and ... make sure that that money gets spent in technology and innovation."

CHAPTER 8

USE YOUR ECOMAGINATION

*"I thought going green was going to be a good idea. It has been
10 times better than I ever imagined."*

—JEFF IMMELT

Jeff Immelt does not consider himself to be an environmentalist. Not in the stereotypical sense anyway. He is not the
one who installed recycling receptacles in his home, wrote
radical letters to political leaders warning of the dangers of
pollutants and global warming, or counted the seconds the
water ran when he was brushing his teeth.

"I never had a big idealistic bent toward the environment,"
says Immelt.

Yet he has orchestrated since 2004 the most sweeping environmental business leadership of any corporation in the
United States, doing it in spite of strong resistance from many
of the key people who work with him. And the irony is not lost
on Immelt, who smiles characteristically at mention of the
leadership as if to say, "Who knew?"

Further conversation with GE's chairman and CEO clearly
reveals, however, that the company's green business initiative,

bundled under the trade name ecomagination®, was not an afterthought or an accident. Instead, GE's green business plan is a very calculated public relations and profit proposition—two terms that rarely find synonymous ground in business outlines—written as a new chapter in the twenty-first century corporate how-to manual.

For anyone who has followed GE for more than a decade, the fact that the company is arguably the blue-chip leader in "green" today may come as a surprise considering that less than a decade before it was embroiled in an environmental mess.

Of course, dumping toxic waste into the Hudson River as GE used to do was legal until 1977, when PCBs were banned in the United States because of suspected links with cancer and developmental abnormalities. Not only was GE allowed to dump the waste, but the government issued permits for it, allowing the company to dump PCBs into the river from two plants in the state of New York dating back to 1946.

Years after the dumping was stopped, though, the Environmental Protection Agency ruled that 200 of the Hudson River's 315 miles should be listed as a federal Superfund site—a contaminated area needing cleanup. GE argued against cleaning up the site on the premise that dredging up PCB-laden river silt would only cause more problems. The company also argued that what the company did at the time, years and decades before, was legal and that other industrial firms did exactly the same thing, into the same river.

Try telling that in the year 2000 to the Sierra Club, which, just before the EPA was scheduled to release a Hudson River cleanup schedule at that time, blasted the company in a newsletter, telling members to "make sure GE learns a lesson it should have realized long ago: Whether it's spilled apple juice or toxic waste, whether you're 5 years old or a corporate giant—clean up the mess." Even a popular New York restaurant, River Café, would not serve meals to GE executives in the early 1990s because of anger over river pollution.

The EPA did find GE responsible for cleaning up the Hudson River in a 2002 ruling, handed down just months after Immelt officially took office as company leader. GE did not agree with the ruling but did begin river cleanup before reaching an agreement with the EPA on how much dredging had to be done. From a public relations standpoint, fighting the battle was difficult. Considering the sheer size of GE and its century-long presence as a leading company in the United States, particularly as a manufacturer in an era when rules and regulations regarding waste were so different, the company's past is not surprising. What happened over the next couple of years is somewhat surprising, however, considering the Hudson River issue.

For Immelt, the epiphany came in 2004 during his annual strategic review session held among top company managers and executives. In a roundtable-type discussion, leaders of each company division talk at this meeting about areas of strengths and weaknesses and new business initiatives. As he listened, Immelt noticed a trend. The company that seemed just a few years before to be an old-school manufacturing type, still talking about waste dumping in a river from decades before, had in the first few years of the new millennium begun to evolve into something decidedly more contemporary.

At the time under the direction of John Rice, GE Energy was beginning to make both marketplace headway and significant profits in the wind business it picked up from Enron's bankruptcy filing. GE Energy had also recently acquired AstroPower, one of the world's largest manufacturers of solar panels used for natural electric power generation. And those promising environmentally friendly businesses were just the beginning. As one person after another spoke, Immelt noticed that GE had evolved into a global corporation with a nice big green thumb.

A buzzword often heard in various GE offices is "leverage," as in, let's put our strengths to work for the greater good. The concept is one Immelt practices faithfully. He understands the power of branding and a unified goal and message, and he understands how one division with seemingly different products from another can benefit from direct association with another. So he put together a plan designed to give one name and one voice with tangible goals and verifiable measurability together into something he called ecomagination, an obvious wordplay on using creativity to solve the world's environmental challenges, from solar to water to anything imaginable.

Immelt put an in-house team together to gather customer feedback on green initiatives and study greenhouse legislation, and he spoke personally to many of GE's largest customers and chief executive officers at many of the 30 largest utility companies in the country seeking input and ideas. The result was a detailed plan including scorecards and internal auditing, put together with help from environmental consulting group GreenOrder, recommending that GE drastically increase its research and development spending on clean technologies and reduce its own greenhouse gas emissions.

"I always viewed GE as working on tough societal problems," says Immelt. "So even though I would not have called myself an environmentalist, ecomagination was the perfect fit. I saw you can provide a solution and make money at the same time and ... I saw we could draw a string across the company in a meaningful way."

Immelt's top executives did not all see it the same way in the beginning, however.

Know When to Invoke Power

In a meeting of top company executives later in 2004, Immelt was armed with his plan complete with measurable results, commensurate with GE tradition. This is not a company, after all, that does much of anything without quantifying expected results and benefits. A public relations initiative this was not. Certainly, Immelt calculated the global reputation benefits to the company and certainly he wanted to leave the Hudson River headlines behind, but not without keeping growth and profitability at the forefront.

When he unveiled his plan, however, he saw the reaction of the 35 executives gathered; it was not what he expected. Most just did not get it. In fact, all but about five did not get it. They listened, but they thought it was flimsy and soft, more vague than tangible and thus against the corporation's culture. When Immelt asked for a show of hands vote for who was in favor of instituting GE's ecomagination program, the measure failed miserably.

Says Immelt: "They said, 'This is stupid.'"

Sometimes Immelt accepts a majority rule vote for advice from his leading lieutenants but typically that is when he personally does not have such a strong gut feeling one way or another as he did about ecomagination. He feels he can get away with flexing his power a handful of times each year and understands the necessity of doing so occasionally to keep proper balance in place.

"There's about five times a year with that group that I say, 'Hey guys, here's where we're going, get in line.' If you did it six times, they would leave. And if you did it three times, there'd be anarchy," Immelt says.

Overruling the group, Immelt led the company to launch its ecomagination initiative in 2005. Constructed under the tagline, "a GE commitment," the business initiative is designed to "help meet customer demand for more energy-efficient products and to drive reliable growth for GE, growth that delivers for investors long term" by investing in innovative solutions to environmental challenges. GE's five primary commitments in the business initiative are:

1. Increase revenues through ecomagination products to a goal of $25 billion in 2010.
2. Double investment in research and development for cleaner technologies from $700 million in 2005 to $1.5 billion in 2010.
3. Reduce greenhouse gas emissions and improve overall company energy efficiency.
4. Reduce water use and improve water reuse.
5. Keep the public informed.

With low U.S. fuel prices, an active debate over the validity of global warming, and the greater public focused more on global security and war with active military engagements ongoing in Iraq and Afghanistan, the environment was not such a hot topic in 2005. Yet Immelt dove in anyway, pushing one of the world's largest companies to shift directions in the twenty-first century from reactive industrial giant to a proactive environmental change agent. GE executives who voted no for the initiative quickly lined up behind the movement, understanding that it was going forward with or without them.

"We've got a good team that knows when to lead, and they also know when to follow, and that's a real trick," says Immelt.

Among those who supported ecomagination all along was John Rice. His energy division was behind the wind and solar acquisitions, and he was a driving force to fast growth for ecomagination through his leadership of GE's infrastructure division beginning in 2005 (he now leads the repackaged technology infrastructure division, one of the company's four business groups).

Like Immelt, the 51-year-old Rice never considered himself an environmental activist. A company director since 1992, Rice began his career at GE in 1978 as a member of the financial management program after receiving a degree in economics from Hamilton College in Clinton, New York. Rice got to know Immelt when working under him in customer service at GE Appliances in the 1980s.

"Jeff was running the service business, and I was working for him," recalls Rice. "I had a business that was really struggling, but I saw then what I see today. I saw somebody who expected me to figure it out and was focused on the right results and very supportive and willing to do anything I needed, help with a customer ... you name it. Any kind of support needed to get the job done, he would be there.

"Some people you work for," says Rice, "you are afraid to take them a problem. When you take Jeff a problem, he always wants to be a part of the solution. I saw it then. It shaped how I think about my job. I want to be helpful in solving problems and a part of the solution, not just another step in the review process."

Rice lives in an Atlanta suburb, his residence dating back to his days running GE Energy, since that business is headquartered there. When he was named president of GE Infrastructure in 2005, Rice considered moving to Connecticut to work from GE's Fairfield offices, but Immelt gave him a choice of residence. Rice's son was finishing high school at the time—he is now a college student at Vanderbilt—and Rice had just been named Atlanta's businessman of the year by a local publication, and he has served as president of the Atlanta Metro Chamber of Commerce, adding to more reasons not to move. Today Rice works mostly out of his North Atlanta office but he's often on the road, and he also maintains an office in Fairfield for visits there.

"I had moved 10 times in 12 years," says Rice. "Jeff said, 'Work where it suits you best.'"

So much of GE's business is global now, particularly with its infrastructure business, that designating a true company headquarters no longer works anyway. The company's top executives are spread out, using the leadership and research campuses as nerve centers, annual meetings like Session C as connecting processes, and initiatives like Six Sigma and ecomagination as weaving threads.

Rice says that even though he was in agreement with starting GE's environmental business initiative, he never saw how big it could and would be.

"I grew up in the company in the late 1970s and 1980s and 1990s," says Rice, speaking from his Atlanta office, located close to the city's Interstate 285 perimeter highway with a view of Georgia treetops as far as one can see. "So in some respects the first two-thirds of my career was born in a time when we got very little credit for environmental things. We were regularly beaten up and criticized for PCBs in the Hudson River, and we did not want to stick our head out of the foxhole [on environmental issues]. No matter what we did, we were afraid someone would say, 'You put PCBs in the Hudson.'"

Rice says his personal epiphany came when he looked around GE Energy and saw that the company was doing work in emissions reduction and improved fuel efficiencies. He says he began to understand that if the company could do something good for customers and make the world better, making money doing so, shareholders would ultimately benefit. Big businesses like wind and solar energy made sense if they could apply GE's research and development with management processes resulting in a solid model.

"I look at Jeff, and one of his great strengths is an ability to go from very detailed operational stuff to what do we need to think about in 2025," says Rice. "And he has the courage to say, 'Okay, it is going to be the environment. We will do this thing called econimagination.' Since the beginning, it has morphed; we added water (treatment initiatives), when we did not have water in the beginning. So you build on it, creating a foundation and adding stories to the building.

"Jeff is smart enough to get it," Rice says. He said we are going to do this and sell more and make money. That was the most far-reaching commitment because it threw the profit motive right out there. The premise makes a lot of sense. If a company is doing it and not making money, it is not sustainable. Solutions have to allow the right risk-reward tradeoff. Investors put capital at risk in our company, and we have to make a reasonable return for them.

"That's the law of capitalism," says Rice. "If you don't make money, then it is corporate philanthropy. That works certainly, and we do lots of philanthropic things, but those are not sustainable. The world's premier philanthropists are pushing for sustainability ... and that is what we want to push as a corporation."

Not all of GE's customers were taken with ecomagination at the start. Nobody was talking much about the environment, and global warming was still a no-no topic among many of GE's largest energy customers, particularly those relying on burning coal for power generation. When Immelt and GE convened a customer dreaming session at Crotonville in 2004 with leaders of the largest utility companies in the United States, some GE Energy employees were visibly nervous about offending their biggest customers.

Attendees included Jim Rogers, chairman and CEO of Duke Energy, the North Carolina–based power company which derives the majority of its power from burning carbon. A featured speaker at the dreaming session was Jeff Sachs, the noted economist and environmentalist who runs the Earth Institute at Columbia University. His subject was global warming, politically sensitive at the time considering President

George W. Bush stirred heavy debate with his much-discussed view that he is not sure whether global warming is the result of human actions or a natural occurrence. Immelt even suggested during the dreaming session that the group discuss public policy on greenhouse gases, showing the organization it is, "OK to stick your neck out and even to make customers a little bit uncomfortable."

"There were plenty of guys on our energy team who hated this in the beginning because half of their customers were saying they hated it," said Immelt. "We just kept talking: 'Here's where we're going. Here's why we think it's good for both of us. And it's going to come some day anyhow, so let's get ahead of it.'"

When GE launched ecomagination, the company went to the world's largest environmental concern groups, including some former adversaries, seeking to make a hat-in-hand deal: We can and will do more to support your mission if you will work with us. Many environmental groups responded, recognizing that few if any global companies have the business prowess and global presence of GE, which works in almost 150 different countries with hundreds of different businesses and thousands of different products. Not to mention that GE operates one of the best-funded corporate research centers in the world.

Explains Rice: "These are big problems to solve, and you can't solve them if you shut big companies out of the game. You need to attract capital to global warming. You need to attract capital to solve the big environmental problems, but you are not going to do that if every time a big company with capital to deploy gets punched in the nose for something that happened 20 years ago.

"So we had an epiphany, and some environmental groups had an epiphany too," says Rice. "It was that a company like GE is trying to get it right, and if we work with them maybe we can get something done. The two dynamics most compelling were that we and significant environmental groups could get together because we both need each other to solve these problems. It works through the application of basic capitalism, that is, if you make more money, you attract more capital and ultimately create a sustainable effort."

Many environmental groups immediately got it, like the Pew Center on Climate Change. Briefed on the program before its launch, organization president Eileen Claussen said at the time that a company the size of GE entering the foray of global warming represented an act of courage. Others wanted to wait for results, but three years later, critics were hard to find. GE's green businesses were achieving double-digit growth and making global headlines. Among the company's 75 notable eco products by 2008 were the hybrid locomotive and wind turbines.

"One of the things that I'm trying to do inside the company is get these 75 products up to about 200 products," Immelt says.

To do that, GE has to find ways to test and learn rapidly. He is pushing the company to do more user interface, hoping to duplicate at GE some of the same success experienced by Apple founder and CEO Steven Jobs, known for getting "products in the hands of customers" and letting them "in some ways define the usage in terms of where they go."

Let the Light Shine

Much of GE's green product progress is driven at GE's Global Research Center, credited in breakthroughs with products including organic light emitting diodes (OLEDs) and the electrical smart grid infrastructure. Each of the concepts fits into GE's ecomagination process because each has an energy conservation tool that holds the promise of contributing to sweeping global change while also meeting the company's future revenue and profits plans.

Under GE's ecomagination operating rhythm, the chairman's office—Immelt—has direct oversight of such projects. He receives reviews including all metrics and customer activities from the ecomagination advisory board, which includes Little. A designated group of GE executives and managers designated the ecomagination team runs the program, working directly with Immelt. The ecomagination team has managerial oversight over the three company groupings designed to create and foster ecomagination initiatives, including global research, health and energy, and remaining GE businesses.

On a project like the development of OLEDs the research center role is to develop a cross-functional team capable of considering all aspects of product development, manufacturing needs, and potential applications across the GE business family. Throughout the process, potential environmental benefits—in this case, primarily energy savings—are tabulated for reports along with research and development progress. With OLEDs, the company is seeking to provide the twenty-first century's solution to efficient, flexible lighting that Edison provided a century before with the incandescent light bulb. OLEDs are thin sheets of polymers or plastic materials that light up when an electrical charge is applied, and they are being heavily invested in by companies other than GE, including competitors Siemens and Philips, because of promising consumer qualities. OLEDs are already being used in televisions and cell phones, but potential uses for the longer term are seemingly limitless.

Considered by industry watchers to be a product that will change lighting the way the Apple's iPod changed music—but on a much larger scale since commercial and consumer lighting is a much larger market—OLEDs are expected to one day change our light patterns by diffusing light from the conventional single sources of small, incandescent bright bulbs. GE researchers say they could conceivably produce OLED wallpaper, creating illuminated walls, since the material is flexible, and OLED window blinds, able to be lifted when there's daylight and be pulled down at night for lighting. And ceilings, typically lighted with a design of single bulbs, would be a sheet of light evenly distributing illumination throughout.

GE has made significant contributions to development of OLEDs in terms of life expectancy, cost, and brightness. Considering GE's history in lighting—Edison did, after all, invent the light bulb—and plastics, which OLEDs are made from, one might expect the company to be a leader in the product's development. The competitive logjam for the product, however—the reason OLEDs cost too much for the average consumer and the reason none of the other companies investing in OLEDs has raced into the marketplace—has been manufacturing difficulty. The lighting technology existed, but the ability to make large quantities of it outside of a laboratory did not.

That's where Immelt investment and commitment to the cross-fertilization benefits of the GE Global Research Center paid big dividends for the company in 2008. While other companies wrestled with OLED technology, GE had deep resources and a research center designed to cultivate inventions to draw upon in making a machine to produce an affordable manufacturing process for the sheets of lighting. So in 2004, GE found a partner, Energy Conversion Devices (ECD Ovonics), which specializes in the manufacturing of its proprietary thin-film solar laminates used to convert sunlight to energy in the same way larger panels do.

Together, the companies submitted a proposal to a government agency seeking to fund high-risk technology development. More than four years passed, but engineers working on the OLED team developed in a nondescript, windowless building of corrugated steel located on the pastoral grounds of the GE upstate New York research center a machine that makes OLEDs in sheets. The invention is a mechanized roll-to-roll manufacturing process similar to a newspaper printing press, allowing for mass production of the big, glowing sheets of plastic.

Before GE's manufacturing breakthrough, OLEDs were made with a costly, slow manufacturing process known as vacuum deposition. GE's machine uses a much simpler process, effectively integrating the light emitting diodes into plastic the same way ink is stamped on newsprint. In late 2008, GE was planning to put OLEDs on sale commercially as early as 2010, with the understanding that the first generations of the product would be more affordable in commercial applications than in consumer ones. Still, Immelt, Little, and the company's ecomagination team could hardly contain their enthusiasm over the OLED progress as affirmation that the company was capable of changing the world with self-generated innovation that holds infinite profit potential.

"This probably would not have happened before Jeff," says Little.

Drive Change (and Provide the Solutions)

Another green energy project hoped to make GE a twenty-first century solutions provider is its electric smart grid and associated products which promise to manage the electrical flow to both appliances and homes in general, allowing consumers to save and conserve on electricity and allowing electric utilities to better manage flow.

Take the average household refrigerator as an example. In dormant hours, a refrigerator's energy consumption can be reduced by as much as 40 percent while maintaining roughly the same desired temperatures if electricity to the unit is shut down. With GE's smart grid, the utility could be directly connected to the refrigerator, just as it could be directly connected to the power of all consumer homes, interfacing with user trends and desires to manage electrical flow, providing dollar and power availability savings. An example of the grid and the energy-smart refrigerator are already in demonstration at GE's Global Research Center, and Immelt says that it won't be long before the consumer will see such eco-friendly products at work.

"The team doesn't know [the smart refrigerator] is going to be launched next May [2008], but I do," said Immelt, in late 2007. "I don't know how many of these we'll actually make, but I think it's important to get these technologies out in the marketplace."

To facilitate its smart grid business, GE joined hands in cooperation with Internet solutions provider Google. Seemingly, the two companies would have little in common in the twenty-first century. Google traded on average in 2008 at a stock price of $400, has fewer than 20,000 employees, and essentially operates on a single business platform—technology. GE traded at a stock price in the $20s, has more than 300,000 employees worldwide, and operates in multiple businesses, from finance to aviation to energy.

But Immelt and Google executives, including CEO Eric Schmidt and founders Sergey Brin and Larry Page, discovered that they had some complementary strengths and interests in technology. Specifically, GE and Google made a pact in 2008 to cooperate in two areas: public policy lobbying and technology collaboration.

The concept is to improve electricity-infrastructure efficiency through advanced networking technology which provides better service to customers and reduces carbon dioxide pollution globally through reduced demand via the smart grid. Since GE owns or has access to, through its energy business and partnerships, vast rights of way on the electrical grid and is expanding this presence almost daily, the company wants to be the infrastructure leader in the new century with its intelligent, energy-saving system.

And Google, through its Google.org initiative which aims to "use the power of information and technology to address the global challenges of our age" including climate change, poverty, and emerging disease had already invested tens of millions of dollars in wind, solar, and enhanced geothermal start-up companies. In 2007, Google.org filed a patent for a floating data center that would be powered primarily by wave energy, so its partnership with GE for energy initiatives and technology partnerships was not far-fetched at all.

For GE and Google's electrical grid rebuilding plan to more quickly succeed in the United States, however, the program needs the cooperation of Washington. America's electrical system is based on, according to Schmidt, an "old-style industrial model." The government must assist this more contemporary infrastructure advancement so that the United States can continue to be a world leader.

The federal government is not new to funding electrical infrastructure, of course. When most urban residents had electrical service in the United States by the late 1930s, almost none of the country's rural residents did because utility companies, many of them private, could not afford to run power lines to the far reaches, across thousands of acres of land populated by few residents. U.S. President Franklin D. Roosevelt believed that if U.S. farmers and other rural residents could not afford electricity, the government's duty was to provide it for them, so in 1935 he gained passage of a bill establishing the Rural Electric Administration, created for the sole purpose of bringing electricity to rural areas. The infrastructure investment is credited by many historians as one of a few signature moments in America's emergence as an economic power following the Great Depression. In 2008, when Schmidt and Immelt sat together onstage in California during Google's Zeitgeist conference to announce the partnership between Google and GE, the country had ample capacity in its grid for the moment but certainly not for the future. The argument was launched that America's grid was neither good enough today from a technology standpoint nor sufficient to serve into the future.

"There has to be more capacity," said Immelt, who bantered onstage with Schmidt about America's energy challenge as former U.S. vice president turned environmental activist Al Gore sat listening in the front row. "There has to be more transmission and production."

The more Schmidt and Immelt talked, the more the logic for the partnership became obvious. GE's strength is making the hardware needed to retrofit the nation's electrical grid, including wind turbines, metering switches, and intelligent chip technology reaching from a consumer's refrigerator to the brain center of the controlling utility. Google's strength is software, applying its interactive network technologies to the smart grid. If fully employed, benefits of the smart grid are twofold:

1. Utilities can more efficiently manage electricity on the grid.
2. Consumers can better understand and manage home and business electricity use.

Afterward, Gore praised Immelt for his "courage" in tackling public energy policy on behalf of environmental benefits but the GE chairman and CEO readily acknowledges that the initiative fits directly into the ecomagination business plan which keeps shareholders, translating into long-term growth and profitability, at the heart of all decisions. For GE, the smart grid is its future today the same way the light bulb was the company's future more than 100 years ago.

But for it all to happen with any speed or consistency, government support is needed through means of incentives and direct investment. So GE and Google joined to partner in lobbying efforts to influence public policy in energy but also to work together in technology on such initiatives implementing technologies which allow large-scale integration of plug-in vehicles into the nation's and ultimately the world's power grid. The concept of government involved in America's twenty-first century makeover is an argument at the heart of best-selling author Thomas Friedman's 2008 book *Hot, Flat, and Crowded*. In the book, which mentions the GE chairman and CEO on 11 different pages, Immelt argues to Friedman on why it is not wrong for the U.S. government to aid clean energy initiatives: "Get real," Immelt told Friedman. "Don't worship false idols. The government has its hands in every industry. If we have to have them, I'd prefer they were productive rather than destructive."

Friedman suggests that the way it can happen is by reshaping the market through the types of public policy that GE and Google are pushing for, including incentives for power companies to buy energy from cleaner sources while working with consumers and businesses to use less electricity through sophisticated switching technologies. This would not happen cheaply, of course, and the irony was not lost on either Immelt or Schmidt that they announced the partnership in mid-September 2008, just as a severe financial crisis was coming to full light in the United States. The United States was undoubtedly going to have to fund its money mismanagement, but Immelt believes one way to stimulate the struggling economy is through infrastructure investment. The plan worked for Roosevelt just as he says it can work for the next sitting U.S. president.

"Actually, this isn't hard," said Immelt. "The technology exists. It doesn't have to be invented. It needs to be applied."

CHAPTER 9

MAINTAIN CORE VALUES

"With global growth comes responsibility. Being a great global company is impossible without being a great local citizen, taking our responsibilities towards employees, the environment, and the public at large extremely seriously in every country and community in which we operate."

—JEFF IMMELT

When discussing the culture of a company with long-held internal convictions and traditions like GE, the concept can come off as esoteric. What exactly is this cryptic notion that one company of more than 300,000 employees actually possesses such invisible and tangible qualities as being a learning culture or an innovation engine?

Mention GE's culture to long-time company employees, however, and they'll usually nod in agreement, as if everyone knows what the other is talking about. They know the dynamics of the company's culture because they live it. And at GE, they are taught it through reinforced training throughout their careers. The company believes so strongly in the merits of its culture, in fact, that it has long adopted a promote-leaders-from-within strategy dating back to the early twentieth century based on the premise that someone who has lived the culture can better lead and continue the culture.

Immelt knows what GE's culture is about because he learned it through osmosis from his father, who worked for the company for four decades, and through more direct absorption beginning the moment he went to work for the company in 1982 and continuing throughout on-the-job experience, training at the leadership center, and formal and informal discussions with thousands of fellow employees and customers. Ask him to explain the culture, and he does not hesitate, delivering on cue that GE is about core values that have been in place since the company was founded in the late 1880s. Businesses may evolve over time, from insurance to wind energy, but the multidimensional company's foundation remains the same, regardless of what category or space it works in during any given period.

"I always tell our leaders that they're GE to the people in this company," says Immelt. "When I would sit around the kitchen table with my dad, I never knew who the CEO of GE was. I knew my dad's boss. And this has a tremendous impact on the 300,000 people in this company. I say my job isn't to manage 300,000 people. It's to manage you. If you have the values, the ambition, if you're able to create excellence, this is going to be a great company."

Immelt says that "generation after generation" at GE the company has stood for three things, which comprise the culture leaders have worked so hard over more than a decade to maintain. GE's core values according to Immelt are:

Integrity.
Performance.
Change.

The many legendary management strongholds employed by GE, from its ecomagination guidelines to Immelt's growth initiative and even Six Sigma, are processes used to get results. Core values are the innate and shared driving forces of people working together at GE which continually guide them toward finding and implementing the best processes. Core values, which for GE include integrity, performance, and change, are the common ground, the likeness among diversity and the thing that keeps many long-time GE customers coming back for more.

"Culture and values really count," Immelt said. "We believe that every day. If you really want to be successful—at GE, or consulting, investment banking, or whatever you choose—it's important to like people and want the best for them."

For Immelt, having integrity at the top of GE's three most pervasive values is not accidental. When he took over for Jack Welch, some pundits outside of the company speculated from his easy-going demeanor that he would not be as tough as his successor. Welch was nicknamed Neutron Jack after all. Welch pushed managers, sometimes lashing verbally, while Immelt more typically coaches and coaxes managers, providing help if needed or pointing them in the right direction. Until, that is, employees show that they cannot get the job done with no valid reason. Then he'll do what is needed without hesitation.

"I consider Jeff a friend," says John Rice, who has emerged under Immelt as head of one of GE's growth-leading infrastructure divisions as a top company leader. "I have worked with him going back to the late eighties in the appliance business. But I know if it was in the best interest of the shareholders, he would fire me in a minute.

"It's not about being nice. It is about being tough-minded when you have to be tough-minded. If somebody is not delivering and is getting the feedback and is either incapable or unwilling to make the changes necessary to do the job, you have to make a change. If you are off your numbers but doing a really good job running the company in a lousy market, you should not have to worry."

Immelt has zero tolerance for an integrity violation made by an employee, particularly someone in his management circle. Welch was notorious for pushing employees to achieve results. But Immelt believes in today's different era that results alone are not enough of a differentiator. The marketplace is tighter; business harder to come by. And the GE brand is sometimes not known as well outside the United States. Citizens likely did not grow up using GE light bulbs or dishwashers, so the company has more reputation at stake in earning its business. While integrity has long been a part of GE's culture, dating back to the values preached by its earliest leaders, Immelt has taken it with his management team to a higher level, instituting a one-strike-you're-out zero-tolerance policy.

"When we get the top 180 officers together as we do every year," says Rice, "Jeff always looks at the room near the end of his remarks and says there is no second chance on integrity. He makes it exceptionally clear every year. You can almost predict in his closing remarks when he'll say it."

Immelt applies the same formula to the Session C strategies when managers are in review. The process has been in place since the 1920s, but each of GE's leaders have added another layer along the way. Under Immelt, integrity became a reason for an employee to leave the company. GE pushes its team to deliver quarterly and annual numbers, but Immelt does not want short-term gain at a customer or competitor's expense nor does he want long-term damage to the company by someone cutting corners. If people consider that tough, so be it. The twenty-first century marketplace, says Immelt, has little tolerance.

"I'm less trusting than you think I am, and Jack is more trusting than people think he is," Immelt said in a 2005 interview. "So I would say we're in the same street. We may be on opposite curbs. Look, I was never a dupe. But I also want to believe the best in terms of what people can do. And if you want to make a growth culture, you've got to have a way to nurture people and not make them fight so goddamn hard ..."

The integrity issue for Immelt is perhaps the single most important quality the company must protect. Since GE's founding, integrity has been first and foremost, and throughout the years it has been a critical difference maker. The fact that GE is a multiple-time winner of the world's most respected company designation by a leading publication is a nice designation, but the fact that when GE calls on a customer, the customer typically takes the call, is far more important.

"We guard our image very closely," says Immelt, who is said to have made multiple removals for integrity violations during his tenure.

What this means for employees specifically is they are expected to follow the company's clear integrity guidelines:

GE's Code of Conduct

- Obey applicable laws and regulations.
- Be honest, fair, and trustworthy in all GE activities.
- Avoid all conflicts of interest.
- Foster an atmosphere of fair employment practices.
- Strive for a safe workplace and protected environment.
- Recognize, value, and exemplify ethical conduct.

Immelt's specific message to employees is this: "You will not get a second chance if you fail because you didn't pay attention to what you were doing. That simply is not acceptable. You may miss a business operation, you may miss a number and still be around. You will never violate integrity and still be around.

"It's one strike and you're out," says Immelt. "GE must simply be an unassailable company in touch with the world. We've got to be clean and strong inside our wall, willing to stand up for issues, but a great corporate citizen with great values."

Commit to Performance

The expectation within GE is that employees will deliver or go beyond carefully planned goals and objectives. During its long history as one of America's first blue-chip stocks, consistency and reliability have been a hallmark considering the company's revenue and earnings growth rate over time.

Neither economic depressions and recessions nor world wars have eroded GE's profitability in the way other U.S. corporate giants have suffered, including Enron and WorldCom or General Motors, once the world's largest automaker which reported a $15 billion second quarter loss in 2008, or Lehman Brothers, once a world financial leader, which filed for bankruptcy later the same year. The reason, according to Immelt, is GE's performance culture.

"We've been a company that's always been dedicated to performance," says Immelt. "And so financial performance, doing what you say you're going to do, there's just nothing that replaces that, and we don't apologize for that. We're a tough-minded, performance-oriented company."

Internally, this means reporting problems first so that they can be solved before becoming bigger, delivering on your word in providing products and services among the world's best. Customers pay a premium for performance, so GE has long aimed to be at or near the top in every business or space the company is in.

Installation of the performance aspect of culture occurs differently at corporations, but neither Immelt nor Welch will deny that it typically occurs as a top-level initiative driven downward through the company by management. Employees will readily adhere if they are provided opportunities, but they cannot push the initiative from the ground up because meeting criteria of top-level involvement is challenging at any employment-level layered corporation.

Throughout the 1980s, the performance drive led Jack Welch to proclaim that GE only wanted to be number one or number two in its businesses. That was a common language cue employees could understand and follow in their aspiration to be the best. If they could not claim that spot, Welch wanted company executives to fix it, sell it, or close it. At that point, however, Welch and GE did not have some of the other aspects needed to drive the company's performance culture. So he created them, rolling out one internal initiative after another at the rate of almost one per year over the course of his career.

Immelt says, however, that the number one or number two premise under Welch was more of a 1980s directive which stuck in business lore than something which was actually and actively practiced by GE in the 1990s. Long before Welch retired, Immelt says, GE operated businesses that were not marketplace leaders or even the marketplace next best, yet they provided tangible benefits to the company in earnings and growth. By the 1990s and continuing under Immelt today, the company's long-embedded performance culture was dominant over such ideals as the number one or number two only concept. Instead, how companies instill a performance culture is through processes which align employees to teamwork of shared goals. Processes are designed to achieve the following:

1. *Build transformation intent.* The organization should show and communicate commitment to shared goals by aligning top-level teams and using reinforcing, repetitive terminology throughout the organization.
2. *Shift the employee environment.* Create company role models and foster understanding and conviction through shared stories and mentoring.
3. *Facilitate personal transformation.* You can't change a person's life outside of the office nor do you want to, but you can help people see introspectively into themselves through training programs and workshops.
4. *Culturally engineer business initiatives.* Maximize the culture benefit and the business benefit of initiatives.

For GE, this is best illustrated by ecomagination, in which Immelt and the company seek to better the world while achieving double-digit profit growth annually.

5. *Ensure bottom-line impact.* Have measurables in place for softer initiatives and consistently track them to parlay them into hard, bottom-line results.

The benefits of being a performance-based company are obvious if one buys into McKinsey research that once found companies with strong performance cultures to "have an 11 percent higher total return to shareholders" and more than a 5 percent higher return on investment capital than that of companies with weaker performance cultures. At GE, the performance culture was so effective during the robust economic growth period of the 1990s that the company applied the processes to many of its dozens of newly acquired companies that seemingly had nothing in common with their buyer, getting far better results than might have seemed ordinarily reasonable. The same is true under Immelt in the difficult business environments he has faced. By creating a team management structure, GE is able to allow the "totality of the system" to overcome the star power of individuals.

Operationally, GE drives its performance culture through company business teams with its operational excellence processes (see Appendix B). GE leaders are expected to clearly establish the value gap (the difference between what customers can do without you and what they can do with you), get costs out of goods and services, simplify manufacturing and overhead, and deliver top-quality products at the best global cost. GE's products are not expected to be the cheapest, but they are expected to be developed with the aspiration of giving customers the most value.

Outside of formal processes, the performance culture is so ingrained that employees inside of GE take falling below expectations hard, no matter the reason. Such was the case in early 2008 when the company stung Wall Street with a rare first-quarter earnings miss. GE's guidance and analyst estimates suggested that the company's first-quarter earnings that year would be around 51 cents a share. One month before the announcement Immelt appeared publicly, discussing the current business climate with no hint of an earnings miss. GE had no reason to lower its earnings guidance even though the U.S. economy was "gosh-darn close" to a recession.

Signs of economic slowdown were everywhere, from rising costs of goods to slow housing sales and increased bankruptcy filings. Immelt and his team of financial experts saw them. What they could not see, because it was a fluid situation happening more rapidly than the financial world had experienced before, was a massive meltdown, involving some of the largest U.S. financial institutions. Few people were talking publicly about tightening credit markets and a corporate evaporation of cash inhibiting the necessary ability to make trades and complete large transactions, but it was well underway, and the first major evidence came at just about the time GE was closing its first quarter, March 2008.

Based in New York City, the Bear Stearns Companies were one of the largest investment and brokerage firms in the world. In business for more than 85 years, Bear Stearns had at its peak more than 15,000 employees globally and a sterling reputation, earning a most admired distinction among security companies by a leading business publication as recently as 2007. Bear Stearns also had the distinction of making the first securitization of Community Reinvestment Act (CRA) loans in 1997.

The concept was that home buyers who otherwise might not be able to qualify for home loans could not only purchase a house but purchase more house than they ever dreamed of through relaxed lending, thus the birth of the subprime lending crisis. Dozens of other leading U.S. corporations participated in considerable subprime lending, but Bear Stearns was among the first of the titans to publicly take a fall. And like the collapse of Enron and WorldCom, GE was stung by the sudden insolvency of Bear Stearns.

Hedge funds held by Bear Stearns as backing for its significant subprime mortgage lending began to quickly erode in value in 2007 as the once-raging real estate market in the United States came abruptly to a halt, but the company appeared to be solvent and pledged to be solvent and worthy long term through the first quarter of 2008. Everything changed in a Wall Street minute, however. Despite Bear Stearns's public pronouncement of the company's strength, customers felt differently. In early March rumors swirled throughout Wall Street that Bear Stearns might be in trouble. Discussion turned gossip into a self-fulfilling prophecy as customers pulled out $25 billion in assets.

To calm fears, Bear Stearns did the unusual corporate thing, responding on March 10, 2008, to persistent rumors with a press release stating, "There is absolutely no truth to the rumors of liquidity problems that circulated today in the market."

Negative momentum gained uncontrollable speed, faster than anyone at Bear Stearns could have imagined and more powerful, perhaps, than anyone involved in Wall Street saw coming. By mid-March, Bear Stearns was at a standstill, out of cash and therefore stalemating parts of the United States and global business economies which rely upon the free flow of money through the largest financial organizations.

For the first two months of the 2008 first quarter, companies like GE faced a slowing economy, translating into slower consumer spending growth, which seemed to be relegated to the bursting of a housing bubble. Fewer dishwashers and refrigerators were expected to be sold, but the problem was manageable. The last month of the quarter turned unexpectedly difficult, however, when Bear Stearns took a fall in a matter of weeks, limiting credit exchange and transactions.

GE was particularly hurt in real estate sales because its commercial property business, a honey pot during the go-go years because the company could sell most any part of its $70 billion real estate portfolio at any time, generating massive profits. When the commercial market froze amid a lending freeze in connection with the Bear Stearns liquidity issues, GE's profits abruptly and unexpected dropped because transactions could not be closed.

Poof, there goes performance.

Inside GE, the quarterly earnings miss went over like a death in the family.

"We were obviously taken to task because it was totally out of character for our company," says John Rice, whose infrastructure division was a shining star in the earnings report. He was not finding any consolation in that fact months later.

"It is a reflection on all of us, whether your businesses made their numbers during that period or not does not matter. We are all part of the same team so you move on but you don't forget. We live in a show-me world. If you don't do what you say, you are going to be put in the penalty box, and the only way to get out of the penalty box is to do what you say."

GE's financial unit fared far better than many companies in the turbulent times, earning more than $2.2 billion in the quarter when many financial-based corporations were losing millions. GE's infrastructure business also did incredibly well for a recessionary period, growing faster than expected. The inability to close asset sales and necessary impairment charges caused a 6 cents per share hit to earnings in spite of the performance commitment, the hard work, and an overall strong company report considering influencing factors.

"We had planned for an environment that was going to be challenging … [but] after the Bear Stearns event, we experienced an extraordinary disruption in our ability to complete asset sales and incurred marks of impairments, and this was something that we clearly didn't see until the end of the quarter," Immelt said.

During an interview regarding the results, Immelt noted that the company's earnings dropping just 20 percent in the unprecedented difficult economic environment was not bad in comparison with peers, but he took full responsibility for the miss, nonetheless, saying he "hated it" when GE did not make or exceed its mark.

In response to the miss and the growing awareness of U.S. and global economic woes, GE's already depressed stock suffered its biggest one-day decline in more than two decades. Immelt's former boss did an interview days later on the

GE-owned financial television network CNBC and went uncharacteristically on the attack against his chosen successor.

"Here's the screw-up," Welch said during his jaw-dropping remarks on CNBC's Squawk Box program. "You made a promise that you'd deliver on this, and you missed three weeks later."

Welch said in the interview he was "shocked beyond belief" and that he would "get a gun out and shoot (Immelt)" if he doesn't make what he promised in the future. "Just deliver the earnings. Tell them you're going to grow 12 percent and deliver 12 percent," said Welch.

Immelt did not publicly respond to Welch's comments though close aides say he was caught off guard by them. Immelt knew better than most of the public that the comments were typical Jack; the more harsh performance side of his decades-long GE culture experience speaking. That is just how Welch might have talked to Immelt had he still been his employee, and he was speaking off the cuff in typical "Jack" fashion. Welch did not yet have all of the facts regarding just how troubled and frozen the U.S. financial markets had become. GE's performance given the conditions might have been considered good. Who could have foreseen what happened so quickly with Bear Stearns?

Regardless, Immelt apologized.

"We let people down," he said. "That's not what we want people to expect from GE."

Welch quickly backed off his harsh comments almost immediately, saying in a subsequent interview run on the pages of *BusinessWeek* magazine that he had really put his foot in his mouth. "I want to set the record straight," Welch said. "Jeff is an outstanding CEO, and the GE financial model is as attractive as ever."

When Immelt was asked during a one-on-one interview in late 2008 about Welch's comments following that first-quarter earnings miss, he smiled, raised his hands, and rolled his head away, laughing.

"Gosh, I don't know," he said.

Then, he focused on his ongoing relationship with Welch, noting that they still exchange personal e-mails even though they no longer work together. The challenge, though, becomes exactly what happened with the CNBC interview and dozens of other smaller things the public never sees, like Immelt being asked over and over again about his predecessor despite the fact that he's been gone nearly a full decade or analysts comparing the company's performance in one era to its performance in a decidedly different era.

"Nobody," says Immelt, "has ever attempted this before. This is almost unprecedented. Maybe Bill Gates turning Microsoft over to Steve Ballmer is the only one close. As famous as Jack was and still is and the different environments we are working in, it is hard to get through something like this with everybody still liking each other."

Immelt says he keeps the relationship intact by maintaining the personal side with Welch, discussing old friends and business contacts and changes in the business world at large while focusing on his role as chairman and CEO on GE and looking far beyond what happened at the company yesterday.

Change Is Good

"Constant reinvention," says Immelt, "is the central necessity at GE."

Nobody understands this better than Welch, who encouraged Immelt to change just as his boss encouraged him to change decades before and so forth.

"Blow it up," Welch told Immelt in handing him GE's leadership reins in reference to the company's business model which by the late 1990s needed retooling.

Change, Immelt says, is the critical driving agent for GE's culture that keeps results coming, regardless of environment. Change is both the old and the new GE way, embedded in the company's culture.

"We have a healthy disrespect for history," says Immelt.

So even though many outside the company kept talking about Jack Welch in relation to the GE years after he left, the company's culture was resolved with the transition to Immelt long before Welch's official retirement on September 7, 2001. Employees knew a change was imminent. The moment the decision was announced in 2000 that Immelt would be his successor, Welch stepped back and allowed the transformation to begin. Immelt visited with customers and worked with management as though he were in charge. Welch yielded long-term decisions to Immelt so as not to bind him and involved him in important daily decisions before he retired so that the moment he walked out, nobody in the company would wonder where he was.

"I was taking over a well-known company that had been led by a famous and excellent CEO," says Immelt. "But I never wanted to run that company, and I never wanted to be that CEO. [But] I knew the company had to change."

Others outside the company did not let the subject of Jack Welch go so easily, however.

"I've answered the question in the media 10,000 times," says Immelt, "in a thousand different languages, 'What was it like? You know, Jack Welch, Jack Welch, Jack Welch.' Inside my company I've never once had to deal with any of that. Inside our company GE people like change, liked the fact that there was going to be change, wanted to do something. And that's a big difference ... in our culture."

Change does not always come easy, of course. Just ask Immelt about his decision to sell and the transaction of selling GE's Plastics division in 2007. GE Plastics was Immelt's proving ground, and he loved the business. He met his wife at GE Plastics, and he made many lasting friends working there. Plastics for years had been a proverbial cash cow for GE, spinning off hundreds of millions in profits and growth. But this is one of the businesses Immelt mentions as having run a hard marathon for GE only to pass out across the finish line.

By 2007, the company's plastics business was hurt by raw material price spikes. The cost of oil shot up on increased demand and controlled global output. And benzene, a petrochemical vital to making plastics, increased by more than 30 percent in price. Cost increases pushed GE's profits in plastics down by more than 40 percent even though sales declined by just 3 percent, forcing Immelt to make a decision. GE is a growth company, built on the three core values. Businesses can change as long as the values remain.

Immelt and GE put the plastics business up for sale, closing a deal with Saudi Arabia's Saudi Basic Industries Corporation for $11.6 billion, a premium higher than the market anticipated. Still, letting the plastics go was painful, albeit necessary, according to Immelt.

"Brutal," he says in reference to the sale. "It was very hard. You always end up holding on too long because of emotions. I knew probably 1,000 people in that business well. You instinctively feel disloyal even though you know it is the right decision for them and the investors.

"I tell my leadership team (on such decisions), 'you can be agnostic. You have to do this,'" says Immelt. "It is critical to make tough decisions if you want to grow. You have to change."

That's why at the end of 2008 Immelt had reshaped GE's business portfolio by almost 40 percent, shedding such businesses as plastics and insurance. And he was not done. GE was planning to sell its consumer credit card portfolio out of GE Capital, but changing market conditions delayed those plans. The company was moving forward, however, with a decision to spin off its appliance unit for investors—a move as difficult for Immelt as selling plastics.

Immelt worked in appliances too, crawling on the floor with servicemen to inspect refrigerators, and he understands how the U.S. consumer in particular relates to the company through its appliance business, which makes a range of products including refrigerators and freezers, ovens, dishwashers, and washers and dryers. By spinning off the company as a separate entity for GE stockholders or selling it in a fair market, the appliance business delivers value to the parent company and likely retains its management team and employees.

"Timing is everything and you don't always know, but if you are a growth company, you don't want to be left holding a nongrowth asset," says John Rice.

Some assets, like insurance, Immelt has been happier to sell than others, but most all of GE's asset sales are necessary for the multidimensional business to evolve, meeting the needs, demands, and growth opportunities of the future. Without change, the corporation will stay the same, and GE's competitors will pass it by, says Immelt. With change, GE is a strong, sustainable entity competing on an evolving global playing field.

"I'm completely convinced that when my career ends at GE," he said, "our company will be compared to totally different competitors than we are today. Change is just happening so fast. Today, people analyzing GE compare us to Siemens (the European conglomerate), but tomorrow it will probably be some Chinese company. It creates a healthy paranoia, which makes you want to change."

CHAPTER 10

MAKE GROWTH A PROCESS

"I have a very different style than my predecessor, but we intersect one hundred percent where it comes to discipline, focus, passion, and a focus on getting things done."

—JEFF IMMELT

Before Jeff Immelt became the leader of GE, growth for the company was a matter of expectation and strategy. Achieved through a variety of means, including acquisition, expansion, and determination, growth was a stated goal to be met rather than a direct result of clearly defined processes. The same can be said for most any company operating under an expansion mentality. Typically, corporate processes are focused on areas like achieving manufacturing quality or better customer service and trained employees.

The long-held practice in business has been that companies with the best products, service, and workforce will grow revenues and profits naturally through action and the laws of attraction. That's the way GE did it, applying operational processes to its growing businesses to yield increasing profits. That's still the way GE does it under Jeff Immelt, but, in line with the company's practice of building strengths upon strengths, Immelt and his management team have highlighted the road to growth with a more clearly defined map.

At GE, growth is now a process—procedural steps designed to lead to the blue chip's grail.

Diagram the Steps

"If you run a big multibusiness company like GE and you're trying to lead transformative change, that objective has to be linked to hitting the levers across all of the businesses—and it must keep that up over time," said Immelt. "So you've got to have a process." To fully understand how growth as a process became a prominent tool in the management kit for GE, one has to go back to Immelt's days of running GE Medical Systems beginning in 1997. Before then, Immelt was working on a high-level leadership apprenticeship of sorts, gaining experience in different businesses, different economic climates, and with different growth challenges. As the leader of GE Medical Systems, he took over a business in need of a makeover and had full charge.

Seemingly, GE Medical Systems was a well-established entity operating in the traditional, slow-to-react space of health care, yet Immelt saw himself as having a clean canvas well-supported on a sturdy easel in a well-lighted room from which to paint. Naturally, the landscape he created came directly from his experiences. In invigorating GE Medical Systems, he deployed as a first generation of the blueprint for remaking a company in the twenty-first century.

The mentality Immelt found upon arriving at GE Medical Systems that needed replacing was one of cost-cutting. Health care was in a slow-growth mode by the late 1990s, and the GE division was suffering from single-digit revenue increases annually. The pattern Immelt drew, beginning with dots that he ultimately connected with a single line, included technology enhancement, global expansion, bundling of services, linking with outside contributors, and owning spaces. Almost immediately upon taking the job as chairman and CEO of GE, the picture emerged again, only this time he had more dots and his dots had more depth.

"Having come from GE Medical," says Immelt, "I had a vision for GE based on what we did there. I was able to experiment there in areas like technology, globalization, and customer service."

But in the earlier days of his leadership Immelt was not exactly sure what the big picture of the growth process was going to look like. As leaders often do, he constructed pieces one at a time as valuable company initiatives. Among his early commitments, for instance, was fostering innovation with investment in the research center and plans to make it another haven for cross-company communication and culture cultivation. Another plan well underway was GE's global emphasis shift.

Throughout the 1980s and 1990s the company was considered a global business leader, but the undeniable backbone of GE's robust profits was the United States. With a focus on the consumer, with its rising income and seemingly unlimited available credit, GE did not have to push hard overseas where the company was not as well known for business opportunities.

Under Welch, GE focused on cost-control measures to drive profit growth.

Immelt knew immediately upon taking the job, however, that GE's business mix needed to change and that GE's business geography needed to change. Growth opportunities lay in China and India and in other emerging economies, so Immelt became the self-professed company's "best salesman," traveling the globe dozens of days each year in search of new key relationships and opportunities. Immelt also knew that global expansion was not enough. GE needed to install what he calls "ambidextrous leadership," a company's ability to be a growth company and a cost-control company.

"I inherited a company that had great strengths for a long time—good risk management, good cost control, good productivity—and I viewed the mission for my generation as not to lose those things but to build capability around growth, which we didn't have," Immelt said.

The strategy for Immelt from the first day he took over GE was to reconstruct the company's base, changing the business fix, mix, and locale so that he could drive growth from there through new initiatives. Among the company's more significant acquisitions under Immelt was the purchase of Amersham. After Immelt was able to sell to the Swiss the company's limited growth insurance business unit in 2003 that Welch had brought in two decades before, he needed a revenue and growth replacement.

Working closely with Pamela Daley, one of GE's top mergers and acquisitions lawyers at the time and who now heads the company's business development department as a senior vice president, Immelt boarded the company's custom-made

737 jet airliner on a September evening in 2003 for a flight to London. He and Daley were meeting with the Amersham chief executive and a small team of the CEO's advisors for the purpose of exploring acquisition.

Headquartered in the United Kingdom, Amersham is a world leader in medical diagnostics and life sciences (gene and protein research). Immelt knew the company well from his days leading GE Medical so he understood the strong niche and global breadth the company held in health care. He clearly wanted the business, but not at any price. Sir William Castell, Amersham's chief officer boarded GE's 737 with his team for negotiations, breaking up into separate onboard offices. Daley served as the deal broker, working back and forth between the offices with offers.

"At some moment, Jeff said, 'That's as far as I can go,' and Sir William looked down—30 seconds is an eternity in that setting—looks up and says, 'Let's do it,'" Daley recalled. "And that was it."

Less than one full day later, Immelt and Daley were back at home in Connecticut, ready to call it a night before work the next day. The deal was done. GE would acquire Amersham for roughly $10 billion, merging the company in 2004 into its newly named GE Healthcare Technologies company. Headquartered in the United Kingdom, the company has annual revenues of about $17 billion per year and 46,000 employees. The company specializes in medical imaging, information technologies, diagnostics, and patient monitoring systems in addition to drug and biopharmaceutical research.

Another transformational deal at which Daley worked on behalf of Immelt and GE was the company's acquisition of

Universal Studios and its associated properties from Vivendi in 2003. The new media venture between GE and Vivendi, named NBC Universal, gave Vivendi $14 billion and a 20 percent stake in NBC Universal while GE retained 80 percent ownership. Operating the NBC network, Universal's movie studio, theme parks, and television business in addition to other properties like the Sci Fi and USA cable channels, the business does about $18 billion in annual sales.

After graduating first in her class at the University of Pennsylvania Law School in 1979, Daley went to work for a private law firm in Philadelphia. She was hired at GE by Jack Welch in 1989 to work in the company's tax division, and within three years she had become the top lawyer involved in mergers and acquisitions deals. Immelt admires her ability to walk into any boardroom with as much or more confidence and experience as anybody there. In all, Daley has helped Immelt and GE shed $35 billion in assets since he took over the company, acquiring another $80 billion in assets, including Amersham and Universal.

The changes were all part of the plan, strengthening the foundation before pushing for growth. Obviously, the changing world economy and environment have had an impact since Immelt took over, but he says he began to realize the growth plan in the new century had become more important than ever. GE might have to revise an earnings outlook or two or adjust growth rates in a deep global recession, for instance, but profits will likely remain with intact revenues and longer-term growth prospects intact, giving the company a decided advantage over competitors because of its growth plan. Or in other words, ambidextrous leadership can be, according to Immelt, a difference maker in the more difficult economy, resulting in stronger corporation years into the future. When the economy grows robustly once again, GE will be better positioned than ever before, he says.

"I'm an optimist. I've always believed the future is going to be better than the past. And I also believe I have a role in that. The great thing about human beings, myself in particular, is that I can change. I can do better. If you can get up every day, stay optimistic, and believe the future is better than the past, those few things get you through a lot of tough times."

Develop Growth Leaders

For GE to grow in the future, the company needed more leaders sharing a forward-looking sentiment. A foundation of new businesses was not nearly enough. Immelt understood that evolution of the company's portfolio also called for evolution of the company's people. No longer was operational excellence enough. So he instituted programs to drive innovation like his newly created imagination breakthroughs program, pushing managers to submit major growth ideas, and he sought to identify key characteristics favorable for growth leadership that could be used for future training and evaluation. The idea was rather simple: For GE to grow, the company should be led by growth leaders.

The commercial council was given a mission to figure out how to apply aspects of GE's Six Sigma processes to customer service. Labeled "At the Customer, for the Customer," Immelt wanted GE to close the value gap with partners, bringing to bear the entire GE tool kit of processes, and to help affect their bottom lines. Since GE Capital finances many of the company's customers, improving their business only makes sense. Thus Immelt says offer "whatever GE capabilities are most important to them and will have the biggest impact on their bottom line."

The commercial council also began benchmarking internally among its best growth businesses and even benchmarked outside the company, looking at more than a dozen companies like Toyota and Dell while searching for characteristics that help leaders grow businesses. The common denominator for the benchmarked companies studied is that they were growing at least three times the rate of the GDP. From this study, GE arrived at a list of five necessary leadership traits:

- Create an external focus that defines success in market terms.
- Be clear thinkers who can simplify strategy into specific actions, make decisions, and communicate priorities.
- Have imagination and courage to take risks on people and ideas.
- Energize teams through inclusiveness and connection with people, building both loyalty and commitment.
- Develop expertise in a function or domain, using depth as a source of confidence to drive change.

The traits were implemented into human resources training and evaluations strategy aimed at producing GE's generation of growth leaders. Immelt says that GE has now added leadership, innovation, and growth to that initial list of five characteristics to create a team training program—among the first team training done inside GE in a decade—to foster growth leadership. A rating system which analyzes leaders in each area was implemented to evaluate traits with the goal of revealing areas that can be improved. Green is given for strong, yellow for satisfactory, and red means needs improvement. Immelt himself has been scored, working to improve a red trait for clear, decisive thinking. (Immelt says that a company like GE can't thrive long term by simply cutting costs by 10 percent each year or adding to new business by 10 percent; high-level decision making must occur to lead a sustainable growth pattern.)

Armed with the critical characteristics, GE employees have a better chance at pushing growth initiatives through the company, particularly if they are absolutely and utterly convinced it is a solution that will service customers and make money into the future.

"We talk about growth leaders a lot inside the company," says John Rice, "and someone will ask me, 'What are the attributes of a growth leader?' One I always mention is passion. People who are passionate about what they do and won't take no for an answer, at least the first time around, can be good growth leaders. We had people in the energy business convinced we needed to be in the wind business and when the answer was not yes the first time around, we did not give up. We kept searching for the right solution and only because we had a group of people who were passionate that wind was going to be big and it was a business we needed to be in did we get in it."

The passion, of course, is what often drives employees to push themselves out of the safe zone. Immelt says that this lack of courage to push outside the safe zone is sometimes his biggest fear, the thing that keeps him up at night. He says he does not require much sleep, getting as little as five hours a night so he can exercise early in the morning and have time left for family outside of the office, but he does stress in quiet moments that the company's sometimes uptight past may inhibit its imaginative future.

"If I want people to take more risks, solve bigger problems, and grow the business in a way that's never been done before, I have to make it personal. So I tell people, 'Start your career tomorrow. If you had a bad year, learn from it and do better. If you had a good year, I've already forgotten about it.'"

Other growth tools aimed at the customer Immelt installed include the net-promoter score, which adapts a metric developed by Harvard Business School professor Fred Reichheld. Using a simple measurement, GE instructed its businesses to track and improve upon the number of customers who would recommend the company to another company by finding out the percentage of customers who say they would recommend GE and subtracting those who would not. The resulting number is the net-promoter score.

GE also gets closer to the customer with its customer dreaming sessions. The preferred method is to bring customers into the inspiring settings of the leadership center at Crotonville or the research center in Niskayuna for in-depth brainstorming sessions that help the company see deeply into thoughts, minds, and needs of its customers. Often, the customer dreaming sessions are held with leaders from a particular business space, but sometimes they involve leaders and key decision makers of one specific company. When the GE Global Research Center brought in leaders in the oil and gas business, for example, company teams spent five days with leadership from the big oil and gas companies, and five days among themselves afterward brainstorming and planning with the more in-depth customer and industry information on hand.

The strategy harkens back to the days of Edison.

"I never perfected an invention that I did not think about in terms of the service it might give others.... I find out what the world needs, then I proceed to invent," said Edison.

Another example of a successful GE dreaming session is when Immelt and the company brought in the nation's top railroad CEOs and their chief operating people for a day-long meeting designed to find out more about the future and challenges of the train industry. Explains Immelt: "We spent half a day grounding ourselves on where the industry is, where we are, what their trends are, and then said, 'Okay, here are some things to think about: higher fuel, more West-East shipments because of imports from China.' We would have four or five boundary conditions. And then we'll ask, 'If you had $200 million to $400 million to spend on R&D at GE, how would you prioritize it?'"

The process helps GE understand the best places to invest research and development time and money so that the value chain is maximized.

"This time is very powerful," says Mark Little, director of the GE Global Research Center. "This is what drives our research, helping us focus on where to put people and resources."

Results help GE meet real growth needs instead of developing and selling products and services the company hopes customers will want. By working with customers through means like the dreaming sessions and the net-promoter score, GE is facilitating growth leaders by forcing key traits into action.

Immelt's tool kit was not complete, however, until he found an organized place to store the steps outlined for growth and that turned out to be the growth as a process map he created. Such plans cannot be scripted or implemented overnight, however. He says he learned from watching Welch wrestle over new processes he installed like GE's patented Work-Out, which uses cross-functional company teams and town-hall style meetings to find ways to take bureaucracy out of the company such as having fewer meetings and fewer approval levels on decision making that add no value.

Welch tinkered with Work-Out for a couple of years, Immelt says, before the process really took hold within the company. Similarly, Immelt did not arrive at growth as a process in an epiphany moment the day he took over. Instead, turning growth into a company process was a five-year work of leadership art, something he began to put on the canvas in pieces before connecting it all together five years later into one operational montage.

By his fifth year on the job Immelt looked at what the company had assembled in terms of growth-driven strategy. The different pieces put in place were working. In his difficult first year, GE's revenues slipped by 3 percent. In 2002, revenues grew by just 5 percent. In 2004, with Immelt's growth strategies taking hold, the company's forward progress gained major momentum. Revenues exploded, with 9 of the company's 11 divisions showing double-digit growth, and so did profits. (By 2007 GE's annual revenues had increased from $107 billion to $172 billion, or more than 60 percent, while GE's annual profits increased from just less than $14 billion in 2001 to more than $22 billion, or more than 60 percent.)

Immelt also realized when giving talks and holding discussions on growth at Crotonville that he and the company had effectively drawn out a road map for growth. He was able to plot out the initiatives, which all fit together, leading one into another, connecting them with a line closing the loop in a complete circle.

The result is GE's growth as a process plan (see Appendix A) which revolves around six key elements:

- *Technology*: GE was founded on technology and innovation but had lost some of its focus by the turn of the century. Needing to drive organic growth, Immelt refocused attention and capital on research and development.
- *Commercial excellence*: The company term is "one GE" which means getting the global sales and marketing talent to work together in a unified, integrated way to parlay the brand to marketplace benefit. Immelt recognized that GE was not as good at marketing as it was at productivity, so he made marketing an aligned company function.
- *Customer focus:* Being the best operationally is not enough in the twenty-first century. GE must provide customer-driven solutions. The objective is to create more customer listening sessions so the company can be more proactive from a solutions standpoint.
- *Globalization:* Become a true boundaryless company meeting the needs of the entire world with a customer optimization mindset (customized products and plans that meet different needs of each area).

- *Innovation:* Reflect Immelt's conviction that even the best company salespeople will be limited without the best products to sell. Innovation drives organic growth and long-term company prospects.
- *Developing growth leaders:* Develop a new generation of employees committed to the company process which drives growth.

When discussing GE's growth process, Immelt typically starts with innovation, even though the diagram runs in a circle and all aspects work together. Technically there is no starting point, but that for him was among his first and most critical longer-term initiatives at GE. Each component though has its place, and the payoff for GE has been significant, he says, contributing to a company annual revenue increase in his first six years on the job from $110 billion to $175 billion and earnings that grew from $10 billion to $23 billion annually.

"I knew if I could define a process and set the right metrics," said Immelt, "this company could go 100 miles an hour in the right direction. It took time, though, to understand growth as a process. If I had worked out that wheel-shaped diagram in 2001, I would have started with it. But in reality, you get these by wallowing in them awhile."

CHAPTER 11

CREATE A LEARNING ENVIRONMENT

"Success in today's dynamic world is based less on how much you know than on how quickly you can learn."

—JEFF IMMELT

If change is the driving force pushing GE forward, then learning is the fuel that makes it go.

Dating back to the company's earliest days, learning has been a core theme and practice inside the organization. GE, for instance, promoted leaders from within as far back as the early 1900s on the premise that shared knowledge gained along the way made them far more valuable to the company than the hiring of someone without that advantage. Five decades later, the company opened its leadership training center in Crotonville to make students out of its employees.

In the 1990s, Jack Welch talked incessantly about GE's learning culture and how the company created it. He is credited over his career of two decades with drastically increasing the educational program at Crotonville and pushing employees to share knowledge with one another like never before.

"Learning," Welch said. "It's all about learning."

Nobody had to convince Jeff Immelt.

"At a macro level, I think learning is going to bifurcate society," says Immelt. "You're going to see people who want to keep learning, especially about scientific or technical things. They're going to be fine. But those who don't are going to be left behind. There's going to be a broad separation of opportunities between those who keep learning and those who don't."

Information Drives Ascent

John Rice strongly believes that Immelt's incessant hunger for information and his passion for dissecting and disseminating it helped the executive rise through GE's ranks, landing at the top as chairman and CEO. As a college student, Immelt was known as an inquisitor, searching for information from classmates, teachers, and coaches about their background and driving forces. He preferred classes with shared dialogue over straight lectures and migrated to friends open to possibilities that the world might one day change.

That Immelt became a young GE employee at just about the time Welch became CEO, pushing company learning, is coincidence. His grasping of the principle is not, however. When Welch pushed managers and executives to develop "best practice" ideas and share them with the group so others in the company could benefit from what was working in one area of the business, Immelt was known to be among the most eager participants.

For example in 1997, when Immelt headed GE Medical Systems, he mentioned during a meeting of executives that his business did not do as well with a customer service tracking process as did GE Transportation, run at the time by Rice. Back at the office days later Immelt called Rice, asking if he could send a team over to study how GE Transportation did it. Soon, GE Medical Systems was performing the process on a level with its intracompany peer.

Had Immelt not told the group he felt GE Medical Systems was inferior in its customer service tracking, nobody would have known. Certainly, the medical systems division was good enough at the process, and the business was in the midst of unprecedented success under Immelt. He could have easily sent a team out for a toasting dinner instead of sending it to GE Transportation to learn minor tweaks for an already functional customer service program, but he wanted his business to evolve, learning from a best practice. So he sent a team in search of answers.

"The philosophy is, 'We're never as good as we can be,'" said Immelt at the time.

Welch talked about learning being a part of GE's culture, but it in reality is more a matter of leadership pushing the principle as a top-down initiative inside the company. GE's culture is about performance and change. Learning happens to be the best way to get there. Learning is the force that drives the culture. Thus, Immelt picked up where Welch left off, furthering GE's drive to learn with an even harder push from the top. He evolved many of the company's learning opportunities and stimulators while adding layers of new ones to make GE a full-fledged corporate learning environment for the early twenty-first century.

Learning at GE occurs three ways:

1. *Formally:* Classroom setting at leadership center and elsewhere; relies upon benchmarking and applicable projects.
2. *Semiformally:* Planned sessions with instruction and give and take.
3. *Informally:* Shared information among employees of best practices and customer interaction.

"Every time we sit down to assess our people on leadership and decide who we want to promote, we look carefully at their ability to learn quickly," said Immelt. "We believe that this is a core aspect of success in today's environment. We see it as a constant theme of good leaders. Almost every great CEO whom I've met is focused on continual learning."

Like all GE processes, courses at the Jack Welch Leadership Center in Crotonville have evolved over time, albeit subtly. Previously, the company's three executive-level in-residence classes lasted four weeks. Now they last three weeks simply because executives, faced with more global travel than ever before, already have less time in the office. Many qualities remain the same, like executives attending the classes stay in the same 190-room lodge, where all rooms are the same. And everybody still wears name tags, regardless of his or her position. The concept is to provide an equalizing setting in which employees are limited only by their willingness to learn and actively participate.

In all, the leadership center has 16 levels of courses, including the three for executives. The first of the progressive executive-level courses is the manager development course, held eight times per year. The 80 or so students attending these sessions undergo training focused on the basics of good business, including concept, application, and process. They compete against one another solving simulated problems via the computer. In the ensuing second and third executive-level courses, participants work on real problems facing either the company or the world at large that perhaps the company can solve. They have to present findings to Immelt, who hand-selected the problem they tackled.

For instance during the second executive-level course, the business manager course, which follows the manager development course by typically four years and is usually offered three times a year to about 60 participants, executives focus on a global challenge and typically travel for one week of their class experience. One year, participants in the business manager course may focus on an issue in Brazil, while in another year participants may focus on an issue in India. Finally, those advancing all the way to the final course, the executive development course, are focused on GE's culture. These executives are among GE's top 300 employees and are considered material for becoming a company officer. Executive development course participants are given challenges directly applicable to GE's culture that they can solve and apply on the job.

"You know, I'm a learner, and most good leaders that I like are kind of the same way," said Immelt. "They are curious. It is a constant process of learning, and then declaration. But you have to declare. You have to say, 'OK, based on that, here is what we're doing, get in line.' Everybody has to get in line."

The leadership center exists for all levels of GE employees, and thousands come through the center's doors each year. Immelt has changed the paradigm for them slightly, making benchmarking a part of nearly every study they do. That way, employees learn through self-exploration, not a lecture. The information and lessons learned may be directly applied to performance objectives back at the office. Immelt says that's why GE benchmarks through the Crotonville experience against literally hundreds of companies each year, including global blue chips and smaller competitive brands.

"To get a lot out of benchmarking, you have to pick up not just new ideas, but the processes around the ideas that these companies have been able to put in place to make them work," said Immelt. "Ultimately, that's what's going to be the kind of thing that changes a company like GE."

Top company executives teach at Crotonville as part of GE's mentor and role model strategy. They have the most experience and knowledge to share with company employees, and they contribute to the performance culture by example. When Immelt addresses young company leaders, he sometimes shares his personal checklist as a teaching tool of "things leaders do," intended to create individual leaders who can excel in the company's teamwork environment. The list includes:

1. Take personal responsibility.
2. Simplify constantly.
3. Understand breadth, depth, and context.
4. Focus on alignment and time management.

5. Learn constantly, and learn how to teach.
6. Stay true to your own personal style.
7. Manage by setting boundaries, but allow freedom in the middle.
8. Be disciplined and detailed.
9. Leave a few things unsaid.
10. Put people first.

The Best Teachers Learn

A less formal, but equally well-established way GE creates a learning environment is with regular meetings of the corporate executive council, a forum of senior leaders that gathers with Immelt four times each year, typically two weeks before the end of a business quarter. During the two-day meetings, considered on a corporate importance level next to only board of directors gatherings, the 40-plus member leadership team is led in different sessions by Immelt. He might for example stand at a board, taking the group through an update on growth as a process or explain how the company can better implement ecomagination. The group might also bring in others from inside the company for information and give-and-take discussions on a particular area of interest to all. And interactive discussion among the leaders is always facilitated and encouraged, resulting in a collegial type sharing atmosphere over the three days.

Sessions last from eight in the morning until six at night. The setting is relaxed, with executives typically dressed in sweaters and sports jackets, not suits. GE's leaders refer to

Immelt as "Jeff," and he gives them a green light for frank talk, though John Rice says that there is never a doubt about what member of the group is in charge. He says Immelt is not afraid to say so when asked a question if he does not know the answer and that GE's top executive typically sits in the audience and takes notes along with the others when outside speakers come to brief the group on selected topics.

Immelt says that meetings with the corporate executive council are some of his favorite company sessions, when the executive group brings in an expert and minds in the group get to work, asking questions and deeply learning. He remembers when the company began its innovation movement, for instance. GE had long prided itself as a business leader, but Immelt says he realized that the company did not know much about fostering innovation. It was spending money on research but did not have the best processes in place.

"We would bring in a professor to talk, and I would take five pages of notes," says Immelt. "One came in and discussed Parker Hannifin's metrics. We were not doing any of this. I said, 'Man, you are a stud.'"

Cleveland-based Parker Hannifin is the undisputed leading manufacturer of motion and control technologies and is widely recognized for its innovative technology practices. After the discussion, Immelt arranged for a group of GE employees to go, see, and learn for themselves. The study contributed to GE's developed processes.

Such a reaction is typical, considering experts brought to Crotonville are world leaders in their field. Immelt does recall, however, hosting an expert on globalization who led to an epiphany.

"In some areas," says Immelt, "we learn our ass off. But we had someone in to talk about globalization. He was good, among the best. About halfway through, I put my pen down. I realized the book on globalization has not yet been written. We are probably writing it. We don't know it all, and we've learned a lot the hard way, but I think we're pretty good at it."

Also among Immelt's favorite learning practices are those with customers and others who don't work at GE. He urges employees and anyone in business to broaden their scope and experience by "meeting and speaking with the smartest people you can outside your company." His personal practice when making sales calls on behalf of GE to people like Jerry Jones, owner of the Dallas Cowboys who is using the company's electric unit to outfit the team's new $1.2 billion stadium in Arlington, Texas, or a government official in China or India where the company is installing infrastructure, is to turn the visit into a learning opportunity.

Typically, someone fulfilling a sales role in business might be expected to only meet and greet warmly, pushing for a deal close. Immelt often stages mini dreaming sessions, however, and urges others in the company to do the same. Face time with any customer, he says, should be a learning opportunity.

"I benefit from the chance to meet and talk with just about anyone in the world," said Immelt. "One of the perks of my job is that anyone will have dinner with me—at least once. All you have to do is be curious about important issues and forward enough to go and meet with world leaders, thought leaders, social leaders, and other CEOs. So I can be out there learning from these people all the time and gaining new experiences."

CHAPTER 12

FIND THE FUTURE

"What we try to do is not run GE as one big company."

—JEFF IMMELT

When Third World economies with immense population bases like China and India began to grow and prosper in the 1990s, nearly every U.S. corporation big enough to travel with anything worth selling globally went running. Many already had presence enough in either Europe or north and south of the U.S. borders that they could call themselves global. But new territory to the East meant new frontiers.

For many years, GE fit the same mold, expanding globally in presence and sales. But when Immelt began retooling GE's business portfolio, he saw a picture of globalization that was far deeper than simple territorial expansion. Take GE's consumer products, including incandescent light bulbs and home appliances. In another era, these products were the driving forces of the company. Conventional wisdom might suggest that globalization for GE in the twenty-first century would mean more incandescent light bulb and home appliance manufacturing facilities in China and India.

If it were the 1950s, or even the 1970s, perhaps that strategy would have made sense for Immelt and GE, but countries like China and India which emerged in the technology era have enough talent to make almost any consumer product they want. And GE does not have the same established consumer brand power overseas that it does in the United States. If the company can sell incandescent light bulbs and home appliances in Asia and elsewhere abroad, that's great. But that's not what Immelt means when he talks about globalization for GE.

China does not need incandescent light bulbs nearly as much as it needs clean water, effective transportation, and electrical grids and service lines—infrastructure. Frankly, the same can be said for the United States, according to Immelt. When Edison invented the incandescent light bulb in the late nineteenth century, the product held the promise of changing people's lives, and it did. Returns to the company for the innovation have been considerable—a century-long run generating hundreds of millions of dollars based upon one primary source.

More than 100 years later, however, the incandescent light bulb is old technology, not to mention the fact that U.S. consumer spending slowed after the turn of the century in terms of growth rates, meaning Immelt and GE had to look in more than one direction when planning to capitalize on globalization. Thus, it is not just about doing business in Southeast Asia, Saudi Arabia, Eastern Europe, and Russia; it is about what business you are doing in those countries that counts.

"A key GE strength is our ability to conceptualize the future, to identify unstoppable trends, and to develop new ways to grow," said Immelt. "The growth platforms we have identified are markets that have above-average growth rates and can uniquely benefit from GE's capabilities... ."

Conceptualization by Immelt led to a much different global expansion strategy from what is typically used by other corporations looking to grow in expanded markets. Besides the fact that the emerging countries have worthy if not superior design and manufacturing strengths, making consumer products requires heavy capital investment for additional factories. So Immelt bet GE's future on what he calls the economics of scarcity and need. GE can get into the businesses with less capital and without as many manufacturing plants as other companies, and growth potential is exponential into the foreseeable future because, even if signs that the once-raging Chinese economy is slowing, the country still has significant infrastructure needs like the need for locomotives and wind power and clean water and electric systems. The same can be said for emerging markets throughout the world. But they require playing on a different field. Fortunately, the personable and flexible Immelt is the perfect fit.

"In China, the government is the customer," he said. "When I go to China, I go to a combination of the department of energy, transportation, health and human services all rolled into one. The leader sits there and says, 'You know what, Jeff? Your train order—you know—you've got to be more competitive. The turbine installation you had in the north is going well.' And he's going down and beating me up like a purchasing manager at GM. I always leave saying, 'God, you know, this is impressive.' These guys connect the dots. The level of connection is very impressive."

The change for GE since Immelt arrived is dramatic in terms of where its business is being done, considering that more than

50 percent of the company's revenue by 2008 was being generated from markets outside the United States and the company's
overseas business is growing two times as fast as its domestic
operations. Immelt predicts that by not long after the year
2012, more than 60 percent of GE's revenues will be generated
from overseas. That's why the shining star of the company's
business portfolio was quickly becoming its infrastructure divisions. Split into two units—technology infrastructure and
energy infrastructure—during a 2008 reorganization, GE's
infrastructure business generated profit growth in 2008 of more
than 20 percent on strong revenue growth as overseas demand
for projects like a $1 billion power project with Algeria and a gas
engine contract with India continued to materialize.

Immelt says that infrastructure as a focus business for GE
came about naturally, from visits with customers and world
leaders. As he talked about needs, concerns, and the future, a
familiar theme emerged. No matter how different the people
were he talked with, all kept discussing the same similar
things, including energy, health care, and water.

"I said, 'This is definitional; this is GE,'" says Immelt. "You
start connecting those dots and realize infrastructure will be
the defining business in the twenty-first century, and we are
better prepared and more skilled at this than anybody."

Company vice chairman John Rice, who led GE Infrastructure before taking over GE Technology Infrastructure in
the restructuring, has been a driving force for GE's growth in
the area because, like Immelt, he understands that infrastructure investments in developing Third World countries are
estimated to climb to more than $3 trillion in the next five
years, with one-third of that coming from China. He also

understands what GE has to offer and how the company needs to sell it.

"Rough math," says Rice, explaining why GE is placing such emphasis on its infrastructure business. "Two billion people that don't have access to affordable energy, over a billion that don't have access to clean water. Then you move quickly into health-care issues after you solve the basics. You have that, and the second piece is a situation where wealth is being created because of the rise in commodity prices like oil and gas ... you are seeing wealth created in places like Nigeria, Angola, Russia.

"So you have a big group of population—maybe one-third of the world's population—that needs what we have to sell," says Rice. "The wonderful part is we can be part of very important solutions to help improve the standard of living for a lot of people to avoid the trench warfare that occurs when people don't have the basics and create improving standards of living everywhere, not just in the United States and Europe. That's why we think infrastructure has a long run, because it is going to take more than eight quarters to fix."

Inside the company infrastructure is an easy sell because people can see the tremendous growth opportunities as well as the benefits of providing solutions and improving quality of life for millions of people. GE's size, says Rice, gives the company the opportunity to tackle very big problems like the fact that China's electrical system is only in its infancy. Outside the company, it is a pretty easy sell, too, because emerging countries have major needs, and with population growth worldwide comes an increasing need for clean water, natural resources, power efficiency, and the like.

"If I had one dollar to spend today," said Immelt, "I would invest in solving the biggest problem today—the economics of scarcity."

The hard part of the equation is that each country has different needs and customs, and GE has a different set of competitors in each country. The solution, according to Immelt and Rice, is for GE to put company strengths to work while improving areas of weakness and recognizing the specific attributes of each area and country they are working in.

Easier said than done, of course, considering that decisions in emerging economies are often made by the minute and the day, not by the month and year as they are in developed economies like the United States and the United Kingdom. But GE, as Immelt says, has a deep bench to lean into to align attributes and dig in, recognizing that the company has advantages competitors do not have.

GE's keys to effective globalization are:

1. Use size as an advantage.
2. Create customer optimization.
3. Leverage capabilities.

The Benefits of Size

The question has been asked perhaps dozens of times by outside observers: Is GE too big for its own good?

Undoubtedly, GE is big. Consider that the company has probably 25 executives running businesses that, if split into stand-alone businesses, would be big enough to land a spot in the Fortune 500. Talk to leaders inside the company, however, and find that to a person they see each aspect of the business as no bigger than a corner grocery store found in any city in the world that has to win its customers over one at a time. The notion is laughable, perhaps, when looking at an annual balance sheet with revenues approaching $200 billion, but true, according to insiders.

"We never think of ourselves as a conglomerate," says John Rice.

Immelt likes to tell people that GE is "just like everybody else," but with more zeroes at the end. He says that when he joined the company in 1982 that GE was considered a big company but that revenues were roughly $20 billion annually. In 2008, GE posted revenues in excess of $185 billion, yet Immelt says it does not feel any different to him from the way it did 26 years before. As long as you have the people and the processes you trust, each unit can run as a veritable small company, Immelt says.

Besides, he says, size has never been a goal in and of itself.

When, under Immelt's leadership, GE shed some of its more old-school businesses like insurance and plastics, the company did not have to double acquisitions made over the same period. The strategy could have simply been, smaller is fine, and we will make as much money as we can with what we are good at. Immelt agrees with that strategy, by the way, at least the part about the company doing only what it is good at. He says, however, what GE is becoming very good at in the new millennium is solving the world's biggest problems, which pays exceptionally well and will benefit shareholders long term who trust the process.

Immelt is convinced from three-quarters of a decade on the job that the bigger GE becomes in terms of breadth, offerings, and expertise, the better the company becomes at meeting the rapidly growing global needs that few companies can tackle because they do not have the resources.

Need clean drinking water for 5 million residents?

Call GE.

Need an electrical smart grid to serve the city of Beijing, China?

Call GE.

Need a dishwasher?

You can call GE too, but you can also call a dozen other companies.

That's not to diminish appliances, of course. People need quality refrigerators and washers and dryers, and GE holds a special place with millions of consumers who have trusted the brand for the better part of a century. And GE has been making light bulbs in China since building a manufacturing plant there in 1908. There's plenty of money still to be made in consumer appliances and lighting, and these areas have served GE well over the years. But there is far more business to be done in the world than light bulb and appliance sales, however, and Immelt says perhaps only GE has the resources to do the full job, offering one-stop shopping in infrastructure because of its size and depth.

Even Jack Welch said before retiring that if someone in his succession did not come along and blow up GE into a thousand tiny pieces, he would be horribly disappointed. That person, he said, would obviously have no appreciation for the enormous advantages gained from GE's deep talent pool and business diversity.

"Everyone tells me about the disadvantages of conglomerates," said Welch, "but when are they going to understand that the strength of our organization lies in mutual development?"

Welch did not have to worry about Immelt, who wants to continue tweaking the business mix so that GE has the right products and services at the right time but believes acutely in the company's benefits from depth. Take China as an example. Everyone with even an inkling of global business agrees that China is a place to be in the twenty-first century. Yet being there is not as simple as just opening an office or a manufacturing plant. That expansion is global expansion, not globalization. To be truly globalized, a company must weave itself into the fabric of a country—not falsely position itself as native but immerse itself in larger needs and solutions.

The strategy is to break up the company into individual businesses and initiatives, says Immelt, and remove size as an impediment to growth. The company's infrastructure business in China has grown over the span of five years from less than a billion dollars in annual revenue to more than five billion dollars in annual revenue with exponential opportunity into the future, according to Immelt. Working closely with government entities, GE was selling an array of products and services directly aimed at making life better for the country's millions of residents. This includes the locomotives through GE Transportation and an array of environmentally friendly technologies in partnership with a leading university in Beijing focusing on initiatives like coal gasification and other energy-related fields and water-filtration technology.

China ordered 300 locomotives, and the first two were fully assembled in the United States, but the remaining 298 are being shipped as kits, with local content of the products gradually increasing so that ultimately it will be 80 percent Chinese. For GE, the locomotive order translates into roughly $450 million but the localization of the contract, something smaller manufacturers might not be able to pull off as easily, is what gives the company the opportunity to continue growing with the country's needs.

"In order to grow like that," says Immelt, "we have to be able to leverage our size in a way a small company cannot."

On visits to countries like China, India, and Russia, or in the Middle East, Immelt serves as the chief sales ambassador, marshalling his many individualized troops afterward to close open loops of opportunity. The company's leadership team, through such processes as the corporate executive council and entities like the leadership center and the global research center, facilitates the cross-company and cross-discipline connections needed to tie the pieces together.

Meet the Customers on Their Turf

Challenges always exist, like finding local partners to work with, and funding is handled differently globally. In the United States, GE has not needed financing partners as most big deals are pulled off by a handful of investment firms GE assists with its finance division. But once GE navigates the global waters, each company business mobilizes much like a sophisticated neighborhood business, gauging delivery and customer satisfaction. That's where customer optimization comes into play. GE's reputation is perhaps more important in delivery globally than domestically because customers don't have more than 100 years of Thomas Edison and Jeff Immelt reaching up under refrigerators in a service uniform trying to solve compressor problems.

Japanese auto manufacturer Toyota, for example, was just a global pretender for its first 20 years of doing business in the United States despite the fact that consumers began buying the company's smaller, gas-efficient cars during the fuel crisis in the 1970s. The company maintained virtually all operations in Japan at the time, not adapting to U.S. culture whatsoever. But the company changed in the early 1980s, reinventing itself on North American soil with domestic manufacturing and marketing that listened to the customer.

Toyota changed many human resource policies, like early morning calisthenics and employee uniforms and adapted engineering to regionalized tastes. The company's first U.S. manufacturing plant which opened in Tennessee in 1982 became one of the world's most efficient, eclipsing efficiency of many company plants in Japan. Progress was slow by United States business standards, but by 2008 Toyota had become the world's largest and most profitable automaker. The strategy is similar to what GE employs globally, removing levels of bureaucracy to facilitate localization.

Says Immelt: "We decentralize decision making so that local teams can develop products, can develop marketing approaches, pricing, and risk management into their local countries."

Immelt has studied hundreds of global companies dating back to his days as a Harvard MBA student, but Toyota case studies rank among the top five he comes back to, in large part because of the effective overseas transfer. Toyota evolved over 50 years while maintaining its culture, the pursuit of continual improvement. That's why in 2006, GE Energy was building a customer application center in Singapore designed to provide customers with educational programs, training, and hands-on operation through a simulated environment of plant control software and asset management equipment. That's why GE Transportation integrated itself into the Chinese market with an established, localized presence rather than with just closing transactions for locomotives. And that's why GE aligned with many foreign manufacturing partners it previously had no relationship with.

"For the future, there's big demand for what we do," says Rice, whose infrastructure business plays a major role in global product and service fulfillment. "There's still plenty of challenge left because we have to figure out what the right combination is that works ... and how you bring it to market may be different everywhere. But what has happened under Jeff's leadership is the ability to take advantage of our scale, the way we design jet engines and gas turbines and sophisticated health technology, take advantage of scale and global reach, and bring the best technologies to market. Then, we operate like the local store.

"In India we want to be viewed like an Indian company," he says. "In China we want to be viewed as a Chinese company, and it is an artful balance sometimes, and we don't always get it right. But if we balance size and scale with ability to deliver globally like we've been around for a thousand years, we solve problems."

Necessities to being a good local business globally, according to Immelt and Rice, include:

1. Work well with different people.
2. Understand different funding solutions.
3. Be adaptable to low-cost manufacturing.

Leverage to Advantage

The secret to maximizing size as an advantage, says Immelt, is leverage. Not leverage in the way of finance, but leverage in the way of developing cross-business synergies. In a multi-business company like GE, says Immelt, the idea is that each of the different pieces becomes stronger than it would be as a stand-alone if synergies are leveraged from one to another.

To grow in GE's infrastructure segment, for example, Immelt implemented a vertical business strategy, creating cross-company teams from GE businesses like rail, water, energy, and finance to find common ground among unified selling and multilateral solutions. Much like a large insurance company having specialists in multiple areas who sell under a single umbrella, GE migrated toward its "one customer" process by leveraging its multiple assets into a greater strength.

"Our businesses are closely integrated," said Immelt. "They share leading-edge business initiatives, excellent financial disciplines, a tradition of sharing talent and best practices, and a culture whose cornerstone is absolutely unyielding integrity. Without these powerful ties, we could actually merit the label 'conglomerate' that people often inaccurately apply to us. That word does not apply to GE... . What we have is a company of diverse benefits whose sum is truly greater than the parts."

Sometimes, the integrated business process at GE is obvious. Sometimes, however, it is subtle and not obvious to outsiders. The best example probably occurred during the summer of 2008 when GE and its media business NBC took center stage during broadcast and promotion of the Olympic games in Beijing, China.

Dating back to the Jack Welch era, cries have repeatedly come for GE to sell NBC and get out of the low-margin media business. Welch insisted that selling NBC was never an option he considered through several lean years in the 1990s when NBC lagged behind competitors ABC and CBS. Immelt has steadfastly made the same claim during his leadership, even when the network slipped in early 2008 to fourth in the overall ratings behind ABC, CBS, and Fox and he took over as chairman of the NBC board, hoping to infuse more of GE's performance and change culture into the company.

The division admittedly has lower growth prospects than a company business like, say, infrastructure, as double-digit expansion in the highly competitive business is difficult year after year for a well-established giant like NBC Universal. Critics also argue that media do not fit with either GE's industrial or financial profile. Immelt, however, disagrees.

"I always say: 'Look, it's a good business. We run it well,'" Immelt said. "We've never contemplated it as a sale. We don't think about it. We like the business."

Besides, he says, media companies typically trade at a higher price-to-earnings multiple than GE does as a company, and the value of NBC Universal keeps going up, particularly in light added brands like The Weather Channel and Mexico's Telemundo. Before the Olympics, conventional investment wisdom said that NBC Universal was already worth more than $40 billion. After the Olympics, putting a fair value on GE's returned benefit alone from owning the network which held all primary broadcast rights was difficult, if not impossible, because the network and the parent company benefitted well beyond the balance sheet.

From a monetary standpoint, NBC expects to make a slight profit from the Olympics when all tabulations are in, but not much more considering its billion dollar investment. Still, NBC Universal made a double-digit profit in the third quarter of 2008 and won respect from nearly the entire media-watching world, including competitors, with its Olympic programming. The games were arguably the hottest network television event of the year, with record performances by swimmer Michael Phelps and sprinter Usain Bolt drawing ratings which beat expectations by more than 20 percent.

Each night an average of 30 million viewers tuned in to NBC, while millions more watched Olympic programming on network partner stations like MSNBC, and another 30 million Internet surfers visited NBC's unique Olympics Web site. The brand benefit to NBC alone is incalculable, but Immelt says that only begins to tell the story of how GE, NBC's parent company, made out on the games. The "ancillary benefits," he says, will pay for years to come.

The locale, of course, was perfect since China weighs heavily into GE's big bet on the future. Coordination for broadcast, security, and event planning required extensive work with leading Chinese officials, GE's primary customer in the country. The company also had a world showcase for hosting 2,000 of its biggest customers. Other sponsoring corporations had the opportunity as well, but their television network was not in charge, giving GE more direct ownership and involvement. GE also launched its most ambitious global advertising campaign ever around the games, sending the message that the company is a worldwide player on the most pressing issues, like solar and wind power.

The company's big punch, however, comes from the fact that it earned directly $700 million of business from and around the Olympics, ranging from sales of power equipment and equipment-serving sporting venues. It also is positioned to do millions to billions more in the future. The average investor may not see, for instance, that as China emerged on the world stage during the 2008 Olympics, longer-term demand for business and tourism travel to the country took a quantum leap forward.

If airline travel to Asia expands as a result, GE will be well positioned to grow, considering that Boeing has estimated that China's development will create demand for $340 billion worth of new jetliners during the next two decades. GE makes jet engines used on many of Boeing's aircraft. Most notably, GE Aviation's new GenX mid- and long-range jet engine was selected by Boeing in 2004 for its Dreamliner. In GE's ecomagination plans, the GenX turbofan improves performance through reduced weight and maintenance. In GE's long-range plans, potential orders can be substantial once Boeing makes its move.

"We're spending tens of millions of dollars on a jet engine design that someday will replace the engine that is on the Boeing

737—when Boeing decides when to replace that plane," says John Rice. "They are still making that decision, and we're investing for the replacement. And a decision on when exactly to replace it hasn't been made, but that is what you have got to do to get those types of transactions."

How owning NBC and sponsoring the Olympics fits into jet engine orders may seem like a stretch in the bottom-line business world but Immelt and Rice believe that the long-term payoffs will come as GE's strategies leverage a multitude of company strengths and applications under one global corporate emblem and pay off. These are not qualities investors are used to valuing, perhaps, since to date, there has not really been a template. GE is betting however, that its strategy will create short-term results and long-term opportunity in a way that's not been done before.

"Size gives you the ability to invest for the long term and not be worried if you are going to be able to make payroll," says Rice. "Like lots of other companies, we have to balance the short term and the long term. Our investors expect us to deliver on short term and deliver the next generation jet engine which will take 10 years to do, so our job is to strike the right balance. Jeff talks constantly to our leadership team about that balance.

"We spend billions a year in research and development that is not going to help this year or next year … to have a jet engine business, a jet turbine business, or a health-care business. You have to do both: spend on items that will deliver short term and ones that will play out over the next 10 to 15 years. Size allows us to do that."

The future of course is not just on foreign soil. Hardly, says Immelt. Wind energy is one of the fastest-growing energy sources in the United States, and the company's joining with Google to promote public policy in regard to the nation's outdated, inefficient energy system is all about resources in its infrastructure businesses. And U.S. regions in the South, Midwest, and Far West all grappled with water shortages over the past few years. The list is long for almost any country in the world, and GE has emerged in the early twenty-first century with its remade business mix as the preeminent infrastructure company, with some $60 billion in annual sales in the category and some ideas that this number might double sooner rather than later.

"Whether it's in emerging markets or the developed world, there will be about $5 trillion invested in the next six or seven or eight years in infrastructure," said Immelt. "And one of the things I learned in business school is that if you want to grow, hang around people that are spending money. It's one of those things that always works, and so we hang around people that are spending money, and right now they're investing in infrastructure."

CHAPTER 13

PLANT MANY SEEDS

"We can't have every great idea, but if we can get other people to plug into us, we can do some great things."

—JEFF IMMELT

Entrepreneurs or firms with entrepreneurial spirit are constantly searching for the next big thing. They want to find the next solution to the global transportation problem or the next dominant Internet and communications tool or the next big cure for a terrible disease or world famine. They are also searching for smaller things with massive transforming powers, like an easy, inexpensive way to remove salt from ocean water or an affordable battery with enough charge to power an entire household for a week.

The long-held theory about big companies like GE is that they are too big to be able to monitor and invest in the venture business and are therefore better off watching such developments bubble up from the ground and making a buy with cash once the business becomes a real thing. Realistically, though, it usually does not work out that way. By the time Microsoft was off and running, nobody could catch it. The same can be said for Intuit, the software company with just a handful of employees in the early 1980s that could not even pay its bills but was an unaffordable shooting star selling multiple products around the world less than a decade later.

Sears executives in the 1980s probably wish they had known more about selling on the Internet or investing in a start-up like Jeff Bezos's Amazon.com. And General Motors executives from the 1980s probably wish now that they had not killed the electric car, as they teeter on the brink of bankruptcy in 2008 while rushing to get the plug-in hybrid Chevy Volt to market with billions of dollars invested in it.

That's why Jeff Immelt has a theory different from that of many big company CEOs, including his predecessor.

Several years into his leadership, Immelt began quietly changing the long adhered to company practice that if GE did not own the deal, they did not want to do it. For the longest time, GE was one of the biggest companies in the world with the best management practices—"Our culture is based on the idea that our management approach is right," says Immelt—and the only way for others to play with GE was through complete submission.

GE was already changing in the 1990s when Welch instituted his "boundaryless company" ideals, designed to eliminate internal barriers. Removing bureaucracy to promote the best business practices and ideas, boundaryless company processes taught company employees on an internal basis that ownership was not nearly as important as were results. At the same time that Welch pushed his boundaryless company principles, Immelt was running GE Medical Systems. He completely agreed with and followed the ideal, but now he is taking it a step further by removing boundaries outside of the company.

Immelt's strategy, in which managers were told to compile lists of every company in their competitive space doing something either better than GE Medical Systems or that GE Medical Systems should be doing became a backbone of the explosive growth Immelt engineered as the business expanded rapidly through new relationships. As he ran the parent company several years later, Immelt believed that GE should develop more horizontal business relationships, recognizing that ownership did not always have to mean total and absolute control.

The vertical company, the businesses GE is in, including its core competencies of infrastructure, consumer products, energy, and finance, is one area of ongoing results and development, and the horizontal company, multilateral partnerships with others, is another way GE can deliver short- and long-term results, with particular focus on the long term since some seeds might one day grow very large, becoming a vertical business.

"We've got the ability to plant 20 seeds," says Immelt, "knowing some will be very successful. We can be an aggregator, and we can be like a venture capital firm."

Since GE previously did very few outside partnerships without total control, Immelt had a challenge in changing company practice, mostly in terms of the way managers and executives thought when looking at opportunities. His starting point internally was a natural, with Mark Little and GE's Global Research Center. Partnerships already occurred there when government grants or university research alliances made sense, but GE typically owned the end-use business aspect, and the company was often unaware of smaller initiatives occurring in the field.

Company practice previously was to buy a business that was among the top in its field, preferably number one or number two, rightsizing it with GE's management for performance. That practice still exists, like when NBC Universal bought category-leading television network The Weather Channel in 2008, but what if GE had found The Weather Channel 20 years before, investing capital and providing backup resources?

Map the Space; Draw Connecting Lines

Working with Little and the research center, Immelt and GE began implementing a process for thinking about external opportunities the company might otherwise be missing in 2005. Springing from Immelt's notion of networking based on the growth model he used at GE Medical Systems, the concept was simple: How does GE connect to the outside?

The solution was based on mapping processes which force company managers and executives to see where they need to be connected and how to get there. GE sees solar power as its next big thing in energy, right in line with its wind business. In fact, GE sees solar power as potentially bigger than its wind business since power from the sun can be converted more quickly and efficiently if cost-effective means of mass collection are available. Scientists in the research center have been as passionate about solar power as they were about wind, but finding the right points of entry have been a problem, just as the right point of entry into wind was a problem for several years.

So Little and GE went to the mapping process it has used under Immelt's leadership "maybe 10 times," researching the solar energy business, plotting the different companies participating in the field according to strengths, weaknesses, and capabilities, and drawing connecting lines from GE to the desired end result, thus revealing how the company can become a global leader in solar energy.

"The methodology is relatively simple," says Little, "but it is about getting us externally focused. It forces you to look outside and see who you need to be connected with."

The mapping process helped lead GE to minority involvement with several leading solar pioneers. In 2007, GE took an interest in Colorado-based PrimeStar, which makes thin solar film without silicon, and in 2008 GE provided Solar Energy with $21 million in venture capital.

Before the partnerships, GE had a solar business, "but it was not that great," says Little.

In PrimeStar, GE invested in a unique, lower-cost solution, while in Solar Energy, GE was looking to capitalize on the growing market of commercial buildings relying on solar panels for power. Since GE estimates that commercial and industrial buildings comprise 60 percent of the total roof area in the United States and Soliant Energy, founded by NASA Jet Propulsion Laboratory scientists and engineers, is considered an up-and-coming industry leader in the space, developing efficient and lower-cost technologies for commercial rooftops, the investment from GE Energy's financial services unit was a natural.

"Sure, we could keep buying small companies and GE-ize them," said Immelt. "But we've learned that it's better to partner with the number three company that wants to be number one than to buy a tiny company or go it alone."

Calling GE a venture capital firm would have been a stretch a decade before. However, Little recalls an eye-opening moment that got Immelt and the company thinking and working differently. A respected venture capitalist was visiting for one of the company's patented learning sessions not long after Immelt took over, and they were busy telling him about some of their recent findings. The venture capitalist was not impressed, though.

"He said, 'I've seen 30 things like that,'" Little recalls. "The start-ups don't come to see GE, so we realized we needed to get closer to the ground. A lot of good work is being done out there."

Little began hanging out with venture capitalists as part of his learning and customer responsibilities, and several years later GE had become one of the top five venture capital firms in the world in energy, spreading dollars into new technologies and company start-ups. The company even hired someone to cull the venture capital market, searching for opportunities throughout the world including Russia, Israel, and Japan.

"Their only job is to find external sources of cool technology," says Little.

The concept is simple capitalism at work.

GE, of course, remains very selective. Nothing has changed in that regard. This is not about throwing darts at new ideas, but carefully judging what prospects fit the company's future through processes in place. And when GE invests, it offers support.

"We kill more (ideas) than we feed," says Mark Little, director of the GE Global Research Center. "But we nurture what we feed."

By investing in these companies early, GE does not have total control, but it can offer its resources, including research and development, other collaborative partners, and management tools. At GE Finance, for instance, its "At the Customer, For the Customer" program offers equity clients service through Access GE, designed to share processes like Six Sigma and Work-Out. The company will even go so far as to help partners implement programs and measure results.

"We have the skill set, and we have the systems strengths," says Little. "This is about adding what we've got to what they've got so they have a chance. Then, Jeff says we should be the best at taking a company from $20 million (in annual revenues) to $1 billion. Like what we did for wind. It is hard to imagine Enron ever having gotten it to (billions in annual sales). That's how we can make a difference. Before, we did not have these opportunities."

Now, GE actively seeks partnerships, building several hundred relationships with universities and similar external research groups. In 2008, GE upped its investment in A123 Systems, one of the leading suppliers of high-power lithium-ion batteries. Seeking to capitalize on the plug-in hybrid car movement while also providing batteries for cordless power tools to Black & Decker, A123 was founded in 2001 by scientists from MIT. GE does not control the company, yet is now its largest shareholder. At the same time, GE invested in Think, a Norwegian electric car manufacturer. Such investments without control would have been unthinkable at GE years before, but now they are commonplace. Immelt believes ownership in such important emerging technologies will better position the company for future growth opportunities.

Many of the partnerships at GE occur through its energy division, but GE Healthcare shares the affinity. For instance, when GE Healthcare was developing its new technologies designed to change efficiency in pathology in terms of diagnosis abilities and record-keeping efficiency, scientists and researchers worked for three years. The result was breakthrough technologies, yet GE reached out to the University of Pittsburgh Medical Center for partnership, convinced that the codevelopment of finer points through application would bring better results. In 2008 GE and the medical center formed a new joint venture company, Omnyx, signaling the first time that GE had ever entered into business with a public sector health-care company. The benefits to GE longer term in such relationships include advanced feedback from the medical profession and more swift adoption of new applications and technologies as a result.

In all, new GE partnerships formed under Immelt's leadership number in the hundreds, and typically multiple company products and services can benefit, provide assistance, or both. In July 2008 for example, Immelt put together a joint-venture deal with an Abu Dhabi investment company that pumped $4 billion into a new joint venture with GE. But the benefits and relationship ran much deeper. Based in Abu Dhabi, the capital city of the United Arab Emirates of the Middle East, Mubadala Development Company pledged to become one of GE's top ten institutional stockholders over the span of several years while joining with the company in the new Persian Gulf commercial investment firm designed to do in the emerging Middle East and Africa in the early twenty-first century what GE did in finance in the United States in the latter part of the twentieth century.

"You move more outside the U.S. into emerging markets where there's presumably more growth," says Immelt.

And GE aimed to get far more out of the deal than just financing opportunities. Company businesses did $5 billion in revenue in the Middle East in 2007, a 50 percent increase from the year before as infrastructure delivered rapid growth. With a respected local partner in Mubadala, Immelt expected many doors to open in the future. The local company knows the local laws and needs better than GE might, and GE's management and investment experience can benefit the local company. Like most of the partnerships GE enters, though, benefits will be medium term and longer term. Immelt expected the impact to be substantial soon enough, however.

"This is the faster growing region inside GE," said Immelt. "I think it will grow even faster over time."

Tend the Garden

As GE has grown under Immelt's leadership, in terms of revenues, profits, and scope from its new business acquisitions and partnerships, he has reduced at the same time company overhead and bureaucracy. The strategy of rightsizing is one from GE's playbook used over the years, since operational excellence is paramount for the company's enduring performance. When Welch followed statesmanlike company leader Reg Jones, named by peers as the most respected business leader of the 1970s despite having navigated GE through the troubled, slow-growth period from 1972–1981 when the company stock barely moved at all, he eliminated more than 100,000 jobs in four years. Immelt himself began downsizing the organization from the moment he took over as a tool for managing the difficult conditions that erupted after 9/11. He is continuing the task into his eighth year as chairman and CEO.

By reformulating the company into growth opportunities which require considerably less overhead than, say, running an appliance manufacturing plastics plant does, Immelt was able to broaden the company's horizon. At the same time, he began rightsizing GE under a plan aptly named internally as "simplification." Immelt loves the word simplification and all of its derivatives, by the way, convinced that business leaders should "breed clarity through simplicity," and companies that could be utterly complex like GE should work hard at being simple and clear instead. So as the company expanded externally, Immelt led a move to downsize operations and processes internally.

The plan, typically, was simple: Allocate more resources to drive growth while reducing company backroom operations to improve efficiency.

"Doing things simply is a lot harder than doing them in a complicated way," Immelt says. "But simplification saves time and increases efficiency, while allowing for the free flow of ideas."

Operational processes that consumed resources for innovation and expansion were targeted and eliminated, cutting more than $1 billion in costs over several years as eliminations included legal entities used, business headquarters facilities, suppliers, and the number of profit and loss statements the company generated. In 2005, Immelt's simplification process continued as he reduced the 11 company divisions to a more manageable 6, further reducing operational costs while also placing synergistic businesses like water, rail, oil, and gas under the same heading—infrastructure. Three years later, he took a more defining reorganizational step, reducing the six business units to four.

The move promised to save money, but Immelt says the benefits are greater than cost savings. As GE gets bigger, its focus areas should be clearer. Therefore, he grouped the company into its four primary divisions based on the three areas of concentration, including infrastructure, media, and financial services. The goal, he says, is for GE to maximize company assets in the best way possible by creating a "limber organizational structure" that is "unencumbered by deep layers of bureaucracy."

Under Immelt, GE's new organizational structure works out as follows:

1. *Technology infrastructure.* Building health-care, transportation, and technology infrastructure throughout most of the world; growing globally faster than in the

United States but overall this segment contains many of GE's fastest growing businesses. Technology infrastructure segments include:

- Aviation
- Enterprise solutions
- Health care
- Transportation

2. *Energy infrastructure.* GE's energy infrastructure segment focuses on the development, implementation, and improvement of products and technologies that harness natural resources such as wind, oil, gas, and water. Business areas of focus for GE's energy infrastructure category include:

- Energy
- Oil and gas
- Water and process technologies

3. *GE Capital.* GE Capital is among the world leaders in the global financial arena with an array of services and products aimed at enabling commercial businesses and consumers throughout the world to finance corporate and personal initiatives, including commercial loans, operating leases, fleet management, financial programs, home loans, insurance, credit cards, personal loans, and other financial services. Specialized lending focus areas for GE Capital are:

- Aviation financial services
- Commercial finance
- Energy financial services
- GE money
- Treasury
- GE healthcare financial services

4. *NBC Universal.* NBC Universal is a media and entertainment company. NBC's signature event is television broadcast of the Olympics, and the network has secured rights through 2012. NBCU's primary focus includes:

- Cable television
- Film
- International broadcast
- Network television (NBC programming)
- Sports broadcasting, including Sunday Night NFL football and the Olympics

CHAPTER 14

FIND OPPORTUNITY IN ADVERSITY

"I've been criticized by the best of them, from the Wall Street Journal *to* Fortune *magazine. You'd think that when you have a position like mine as CEO that people would be nice to you. Instead, you're only a bigger target."*

—JEFF IMMELT

Nobody is more bullish on GE than its lead executive, Jeff Immelt.

He knew when he took over the company that it needed a complete makeover. Jack Welch told him as much when passing the reins. But after his sixth year on the job as chairman and CEO of one of the largest companies in the world, Immelt saw from the perch that nobody else is privileged to know that GE had made substantial progress. Portfolio reshaping was well underway, new processes were creating growth, simplification was taking hold, and the world was awash in infrastructure opportunity.

So the chairman and CEO started buying stock.

Beginning in 2005, and intensifying steadily during 2006, 2007, and 2008, Immelt personally purchased more than $15 million of GE stock, much of it on the open market and all of it at an average price in the mid-$30s per share. He bought more than any company inside trader in years, filling his 401K retirement account and his trading account with thousands of GE stock shares. As late as May 2008, two months after the company was stung by the first major signs of the stifled credit markets and financial crisis, Immelt bought 115,000 shares at a price of just more than $30 per share.

Believe in Your Actions

The reasoning for the bullishness was clear. GE was growing, fast, and its new businesses were making rapid headway globally, including energy, transportation, aviation, and finance. The new century had started tough. Immelt had that one good day in office and then the debacles of Enron and WorldCom were followed by a housing bubble and hints of recession, but GE's twenty-first-century plan was in full stride with revenues and profits up by more than 60 percent and business booked and contracted into the future numbering in the billions.

Some problem areas remained, like in finance where the company was trying to shift from some potential trouble spots such as consumer credit cards, but even GE's finance division was strong top to bottom, especially considering the environment. The company routinely applied a stress test to its lending group, determining how a sudden rise of a point or two in interest rates would affect business. And GE Capital was well diversified in terms of both mix and geographical scope so that the impending downturn was not expected to cause any severe internal pain. Besides, the company had endured some of the most difficult years the United States had known in a quarter of a century. With more global breadth all the way through its finance division, the company was better balanced than perhaps any operating in the industrial and finance categories.

"This is the best set of businesses we've ever had," says Immelt, "very robust, very global. I think if you polled 5,000 global business leaders on who they thought was doing this right, we would be on most lists. We're not yet good enough. We need to be more local … and we need to be very adaptable technologically, but we are doing some things that have never been done before in scale and ability."

Specifically, Immelt knew what others outside the company did not know—that enthusiasm for its infrastructure businesses was pushing the limits of what a well-heeled company like GE could keep up with, and the finance business was actually making headway in the recessionary market. Picking up valuable commercial properties at fire sale prices from struggling financial firms like Merrill Lynch that no longer wanted ownership of prime spots throughout the country, GE Capital would resell the bargain assets at fair prices, boosting company profits or at least overcoming write-offs in more troubled consumer lending areas.

Immelt did not know what the price of GE's stock should have been, but he was convinced that shares were trading at a deep discount compared to other blue-chip companies and other companies operating in similar spaces. At a price-to-earnings multiple of just more than 12, the company was valued at less than many purely financial companies that did not have triple-A rating or billions in fast growth or tangible asset businesses like GE's aviation, manufacturing, and media.

In response, Immelt reached out in early 2008 to millions of company shareholders with a live, interactive Internet question and answer session. The objective was shared information in an open setting to enhance transparency and understanding. The format, however, was anything but. Sitting in a GE-owned NBC studio with Carl Quintanilla, cohost of the popular CNBC financial news program Squawk Box, and Chrystia Freedland, managing editor of the *Financial Times*, for 30 minutes Immelt answered a few of more than 6,000 questions submitted by shareholders. The moment was almost presidential, a blend of journalism and control in the name of dissemination, and the overriding message was clear. GE was paying a blue-chip dividend yield and earning $20 billion in profits but the market was more rewarding to many companies paying a negligible dividend with barely any earnings at all.

"We ought to be trading at a premium to the S&P (500 stock index average)," Immelt said.

The market was hardly acting reasonably in the new millennium, though. Beginning with the technology stocks bust and gaining momentum with 9/11, Enron and WorldCom was tepid with many of its former allies that they were growing and making money, often residing instead with companies unproven over the long term with fewer assets and arguably less future prospects. And it would only get worse in the weeks and months ahead.

At precisely the moment Immelt was discussing GE's strengths, Bear Stearns' weaknesses were unfolding at corporate light speed. Everything the firm built in more three-quarters of a century was evaporating in only a matter of days. GE suffered an unsuspecting rabbit-punch blow from the fallout and moved quickly to try to make changes to its financial portfolio to ease similar blows in the future. With billions of dollars worth of large assets for sale that no longer fit company plans drawing considerable interest and with its growth businesses on the move, GE was well-positioned for anything but a 100-year corporate flood.

By September 2008, though, the 115,000 shares of GE stock Immelt bought at just more than $30 each were underwater, trading into the mid-20s, as the world learned the distressing news that its financial system was in shambles and money was no longer flowing among the big money firms. Longtime Wall Street investment stalwart Lehman Brothers landed the first big blow, filing for bankruptcy at the same time that the government announced an $85 billion bailout of insurer AIG. Immelt knew what was coming afterward. Wall Street began holding its collective breath to see what would happen next.

The Dow Jones Industrial Average posted its biggest one day drop since September 17, 2001, and GE's stock was among the blue chips taking a heavy hit, but all Immelt could do was offer assurances that his company was no Bear Stearns. Not even close.

While the Congress debated its controversial $700 financial bailout of the troubled mortgage and finance companies aimed at easing the nation's money, Immelt reaffirmed upcoming earnings for GE and reassured investors that, while the situation was becoming more dire for company finance division GE Capital, which generates almost half of the company's earnings, GE was not expected to suffer unusually in the crisis.

Based on internal appraisal, Immelt had every reason to believe this since, according to Wall Street standards, GE Capital is among the most conservative nonbank finance business in the world. At midyear 2008, for instance, GE Capital had roughly $60 billion of shareholder equity supporting about $700 billion in assets, translating into a leverage ratio of 12 to 1. But the difference in GE is that the company is far more than a diversified financial unit. GE is an industrial leader, and the financial division is strongly supported on the company balance sheet by assets on the other side, including valuable properties like NBC Universal, appliance and jet engine manufacturing, and others which significantly lower the company's overall debt-to-asset ratio to something closer to 7 to 1, depending on asset value at the time.

Even if GE did not have substantial assets on the other side of its business to support finance, consider in comparison that Lehman Brothers had a debt-to-asset ratio of 30 to 1 when it filed for bankruptcy, and Lehman did not have other valuable industrial assets to sell for cash generation like GE does.

Still, GE's conservative finance position gave the company much firmer footing than other diversified financial companies when the crisis hit its stride. Yes, GE Capital had some subprime mortgage exposure after reentering the business during the housing boom of 2004, remaining until troubles arose in 2007; yes, GE Capital had $30 billion in consumer debt through its private label consumer credit cards used at retailers including Wal-Mart and Lowe's; and, yes, GE Capital lost $1 billion on its former Japanese consumer financing company.

But GE Capital's portfolio was diversified by design. Holdings include everything from financing of commercial properties throughout the world including those for fast food restaurants and hotels to the 1,800-plus commercial airplanes the company owns and leases to financing of its infrastructure products, including wind turbines.

"We do boring stuff fundamentally in financial services," Immelt said. "And I'm proud of that."

Caught in a Storm

But as has been the case since Immelt took over as CEO in September 2001, the world was not behaving the way it did for many years before. What seemed true on one day was no longer true the next. The fluid financial crisis situation became downright tumultuous with waves of bad news eclipsing one another hourly. Similar to GE's experience in the Bear Stearns debacle, the company was receiving more bad news with each passing moment of the informational barrage. When it was just AIG and Lehman Brothers deeply in trouble, as it appeared to be when Immelt spoke in California, GE Capital was in good shape earningswise, considering the government's loan to the insurer covered the company's exposure there, and it was barely exposed in regard to Lehman Brothers at all.

GE CFO Keith Sherin was busy working with his staff around the clock in a war room kind of atmosphere, assessing breaking information from within the financial arena as it piled up page after page in the days of late September. He was canceling all appointments not related to the crisis, gathering information, and putting the many scattered pieces together so that the company knew its position as revelations from banks and lending companies grew increasingly dire. From an earnings standpoint, GE was still in good shape compared to other companies operating heavily in the financial space because of the company's more conservative stance, but the damage would be farther reaching than anyone knew in the beginning. Company earnings would take a hit, but that was not the biggest problem.

Financial companies in the United States were roiling. Even Goldman Sachs, one of the largest investment banks in the world with $85 billion in revenues from a variety of services, including investment banking, investment services, investment management, and mergers and acquisitions advice, was suspected to be in trouble by late September. Later that month, it turned itself into a bank holding company. When Goldman Sach's stock price dropped nearly a yearly low with a price-to-earnings ratio in the mid-single digits, legendary investor Warren Buffett stepped in, investing $5 billion on behalf of Berkshire Hathaway, the publicly owned investment management firm he runs as chairman and CEO.

Buffett had received a call from a well-known Goldman Sachs banker on the morning of September 23 as the U.S. stock market sank during a second attempt by Congress to pass a $700 bailout plan. Buffett was working at Berkshire Hathaway's headquarters in Omaha, Nebraska, sitting at his desk while sipping Cherry Coke and eating mixed nuts when the banker asked if he was interested in investing in Goldman Sachs and if so, what type of investment. The banker, Byron Trott, had worked with Buffett many times in the past, advising him on multiple business deals. With Goldman Sachs's stock price down and government approval of the $700 billion buyout seeming imminent, talks progressed quickly.

The 78-year-old Buffett has long been fond of Goldman Sachs, remembering when his father took him on a visit to the company when he was just 10 years old. As an adult working in investments, he worked with Goldman Sachs throughout his career, perhaps more than any other investment firm. Thus, his value-priced investment with federal assistance on the way required little debate.

Two days after Buffett's Goldman Sachs investment was announced, Immelt and GE announced lower guidance on upcoming quarterly earnings and for the remainder of the year, citing "unprecedented weakness and volatility" in marketplace conditions. Immelt said that GE expected in the rough conditions to see, "Higher losses and loss provisions and lower gains." He also said that GE was suspending its planned stock buyback program, holding onto its cash so that GE Capital would not have to support acquisitions by the parent company and freeing up Immelt to pick up bargains in the devalued-asset marketplace. The company also stated that its annual dividend from GE Capital would be reduced from 40 percent to 10 percent, but said that GE's dividend to shareholders, paying its highest yield ever, would remain intact (though it would not increase for the first time in 27 years).

When Immelt was asked if he thought the company might need additional funds to steer through the heavy storm, he said no, stating that the company was prepared for the environment as it existed. GE's moves were widely applauded for protecting its triple-A bond rating which provides the company's low rates on borrowing. The rating may not sound all that important, but GE is one of just six corporations in the world holding a triple-A credit rating. With it, the company can borrow money at an interest rate of just more than 7 percent, while other solid companies have to pay far more, including Buffett's Berkshire Hathaway (8 percent) and Morgan Stanley (10.6 percent). Without it, GE's interest rates would rise, costing the company profits while limiting important acquisitions and funding strategies with less available cash. That's why Immelt said that the triple-A rating was "incredibly important" to the company and vowed to protect it.

In the days that followed, the stock market was insensitive to reassurances. Sensing the increasing distress from other financial companies and momentarily discounting the triple-A bond rating, investors had beaten GE's share price down into the mid-20s, well below the yearly high of $42.15 reached on October 2.

Not much gets past GE from an accounting standpoint. Since the company is a collection of businesses generating more than $180 billion in annual revenues under a unifying umbrella of management, its accounting department is among the most sophisticated in the world. Immelt, for example, is not surrounded on his office floor at Fairfield by operations executives. Instead, he is surrounded by a team of finance experts. Led by Keith Sherin, GE's chief financial officer, they have better analytical abilities than the finance offices of many small countries and a larger budget to crunch. They can work only with what they have, however, and external facts changed by the hour during the unfurling of the U.S. financial crisis, when credit markets seized and the price of commercial paper soared, a key factor for GE since the company fairly often holds as much as $100 billion or more of short-term debt, though some of it is backed by bank lines of credit.

When commercial paper costs more, GE's earnings are affected. If commercial paper becomes unavailable, GE would have to fund rollover notes due with cash. The dilemma is what has long concerned some GE investors, the bundling of industry and finance into a multidimensional company. Wall Street is known to prefer investments in corporations with a single focus because they can be better defined to categories like finance, retail, or manufacturing. Immelt is well aware of the argument made for either selling GE Capital or spinning it off into a stand-alone company so that GE investors can get paid for the true worth of the finance business and so that the company's industrial businesses will be freed for investment on their own merits. But with a 40 percent annual dividend coming from GE Capital—a business unit earning billions in profits against reasonable risk—walking away was neither easy nor smart. Also, says Immelt, GE Capital allows the company to do business it could never do without the close association of a finance arm. In GE's growing infrastructure business, for instance, the company can offer one-stop shopping, financing wind turbines and jet engines at better rates for customers than they could get elsewhere.

In late September, however, Immelt understood well the concerns, just as he understood the unilateral damage coming from the rapidly changing marketplace, which had quickly turned deeply sour. He was already working to reduce the company's reliance on its finance division to 40 percent of annual revenues through a variety of moves, including the sale of its Japanese consumer finance arm and reduced U.S. mortgage and consumer lending exposures. He had no plans for selling or spinning off GE Capital, noting only that any and all GE businesses sooner or later come up for review. The moment NBC, or GE Capital, or even GE's wind business does not serve the company's portfolio, he says, he will not hesitate to make a sale or spinoff, just as he did with plastics, insurance, and appliances.

After all, GE is about change.

Even in the difficult conditions, though, Immelt talked in September about the company's overall portfolio being in its best shape in years. GE had no control over the economic environment, but it did have a business mix including finance that Immelt firmly believed would cohesively ignite in an improved market.

Despite the drag on its finance division during the worst global economic conditions since the 1930s, GE was not in trouble, he says. Not in the way Bear Stearns was in trouble, anyway. And not in the way Lehman Brothers was in trouble. The company could likely have labored through the tangled financial mess without making a major cash generation move, meeting calls on some of its short-term commercial paper and refinancing others at higher rates, thereby inflicting considerably more pain to strained earnings and perhaps even forcing sales of assets at reduced prices. Immelt, though, did not want to jeopardize the company's hard-earned reputation as a safe blue-chip bet, and the collapse of the financial system was causing real short-term problems for GE.

With the latest information in hand, Sherin was worried that seized credit markets would keep GE from getting the cash it needed to fund commercial paper rollovers, which occur on a monthly basis, and shortfalls resulting from asset write-downs. One option Sherin discussed with Immelt was making GE Capital a bank. Goldman Sachs had just done it; so had Morgan Stanley. Those companies filed for and received charters as U.S. bank holding companies, dropping their previous status as investment banks that they had held for years. They did this so that they could access government lending channels like the Federal Reserve. Sherin and Immelt gave thought to doing exactly the same thing in the final days of September, seeking any way to keep the company's money and business machine rolling.

That was just one option under consideration by GE, though. Another option was selling company stock to raise funds. Being a bank meant more red tape, which could slow and hinder GE's easy movement as a finance and investment business. Selling stock into the marketplace likely meant taking even more of a hit to the company's current devalued shares.

Something had to be done, though. The question was only, what?

By Tuesday, September 30, Immelt and Sherin arrived at a tentative plan. GE would offer Warren Buffett a deal he could not turn down. If he agreed, GE would, at the same time, sell $12 billion in common stock, getting the cash needed to weather the financial storm.

GE contacted Trott at Goldman Sachs to approach Buffett about the investment deal.

Buffett said he was interested.

Immelt needed to discuss the plan with board members.

Trott told Buffett to expect an early call the next morning.

Buffett was at his home in Omaha, Nebraska, on the morning of Wednesday, October 1, when his wife, Astrid, woke him up precisely at 6:55 a.m. so that he would be ready for the call.

By 7:30 a.m., the deal was done, and Buffett, still wearing his favorite old robe, walked into the kitchen, telling a breakfast guest that he had just agreed to invest $3 billion in GE on behalf of Berkshire Hathaway.

When the New York Stock Exchange opened an hour later that day, details on the Buffett deal were still being finalized behind the scenes, and the public had not been notified. GE's stock was on its way down again as an analyst at Deutsche Bank said he was cutting his 2008 profits forecast for GE with just three months left in the year. As the stock fell, the price of lender's insurance (credit default swaps) on GE Capital's bonds rose, causing even more external pressure on the company.

Immelt was frustrated, to say the least. With the quarterly earnings report just days away, he knew that GE would post below what had been expected just six months earlier, or even six weeks earlier, but he knew that the company's numbers, considering the severely unfavorable conditions, were awfully good. To Immelt, this was frustrating, very frustrating.

Shortly after lunch, the announcement was made of Buffett's investment, and Immelt resumed his normal work schedule, remaining in constant contact with Sherin for any updates. In less than half a day GE had collected $15 billion in cash and earned an endorsement from Buffett. GE would use the money to navigate the crisis turbulence, buffering against feared frozen credit markets, while Buffett hoped his investment instinct would pay off handsomely.

That Buffett accepted the offer in such a short time came as little surprise to observers, considering that the investor has long been a student of the hefty guide *Security Analysis*, written by Benjamin Graham and David Dodd and first published in 1934. Still in print, the book is one of Buffett's favorite books—of his favorite four books, he says that two are copies of *Security Analysis*, often called the bible of value investing. Over Buffett's career of more than 50 years, he has returned to this tome, which has more than 1 million copies in print, time and time again, and draws upon its advice to buy into companies at low prices when everybody else is panicking.

One case study in the book, updated in a second edition in 1940, relates specifically to GE, known as an industrial power-house at the time. Authors Graham and Dodd noted that the share price of GE fluctuated wildly in the 1930s, a sign that the stock was prone to speculation rather than being purchased for investment. "Certainly nothing had happened within twelve months' time to destroy more than half the value of this powerful enterprise," the authors wrote.

Buffett had the same thoughts about GE more than three-quarters of a century later upon receiving the call from Goldman Sachs's Trott, offering him the $3 billion of new issue GE preferred stock with a 10 percent coupon. Buffett also got the option on another $3 billion in common stock over a five-year period at $22. A caveat of the deal was agreement by Immelt and Sherin that they would not sell more than 10 percent of their personal shares until Buffett divested Berkshire Hathaway's. (Immelt personally bought more than $10 million of GE stock over the previous two years when the stock price was in the 30s, but he has often said that he was a long-term investor with no plans to sell.)

As recently as March 2007 Buffett's Berkshire Hathaway owned just less than 8 million shares of GE stock, a small holding considering that the company at that time had an equity position of more than $60 billion. But that was when GE traded at $39 a share with a much higher price-to-earnings multiple. In the different environment, he warmed quickly to GE's value and safety because it met his value-investing rules for tough times. According to Buffett biographer Alice Schroeder, who wrote the bestselling book *The Snowball: Warren Buffett and the Business of Life*, Buffett-type tips for investing in a crisis include:

1. Cash combined with courage in a crisis is priceless.
2. Don't invest in things you don't understand.
3. Don't try to catch a falling knife until you have a handle on the risk.

Buffett says he did not hesitate to invest in GE because the company is the "symbol of American business to the world," and he had long known both Welch and Immelt, believing strongly in the company's culture, its commitment to performance, and its integrity. Immelt had visited with Buffett in Omaha over the years, and the two had shared multiple telephone conversations, so they already had a relationship.

As for GE, the plan was a complete reversal from its position one week before when Immelt said that the company had no plans to issue more stock to raise capital. At the time, he meant it, of course. The company had recently bought a lot of shares at more than $30 each with its repurchase plan, and nobody inside the company, particularly the chairman and CEO, wanted to let them go at such a deep discount. Tough times do call for tough measures, however, and the company's intermediate and long-term future meant more to its leader than a little bit of short-term humility.

In the days after Buffett's investment, GE was scheduled to post its third-quarter earnings report, and the investment world was watching eagerly. Because of GE's size and diversity and because the company has been among the biggest components of the U.S. large-business realm for more than a century, many consider the company to be an apt economic bellwether for the nation. Everyone wanted to see if the typically reliable blue chip was suffering more in the crisis than anybody suspected. The number showed that GE was nowhere close to being in trouble, with revenues rising by 11 percent to more than $47 billion, largely on strengths in its infrastructure businesses, with earnings of 43 cents a share, a decrease of 22 percent from the previous quarter. Considering the situation, most notably GE's mammoth finance position during one of the worst crises the world has known, the numbers were weaponry against naysayers.

With some of the nation's largest banks crumbling under pressure, GE earned $2 billion from its finance operations, proving that GE Capital, while challenged in the difficult market, was not Lehman Brothers or Bear Stearns or anything close.

On the same day that GE posted its earnings, Immelt conducted a town-hall-style meeting with NBC employees, urging them to "hold onto" their dreams during the difficult financial conditions. He was doing exactly the same thing, pushing forward with plans, refusing to let GE get mired in the financial mess. Immelt was continuing on the job normally, assessing the fluid financial conditions on a daily basis with Sherin and other leadership team members as he would any major company problem, while keeping to his regular schedule and demanding performance.

Even though the markets continued to roil despite government actions to stem the financial crisis from the United States to the United Kingdom, because of increasing signs of lingering recession in the weeks that followed Buffett's cash injection, the public stock offering, and the stable earnings report, Immelt remained completely bullish on the company.

For instance, Immelt remembers the mid-1990s, when GE's gas turbine business was getting clobbered in a treacherous, competitive market. Because of GE's size, the company was able to double down, investing more in the space and watching the competition reduce from five to three. By the time the tough period was over, GE owned the space, and profits soared. During the turbulence of the 2008 financial crisis, Immelt knew that the proverbial low-hanging fruit was long gone from the global economy but figured that GE was better prepared for more difficult conditions than most companies.

"In the last three or four years, [we made] tons of easy money," said Immelt. "Being a triple-A rated, globally positioned company like GE, you get undervalued to a certain extent. At a time like this, triple-A really pays off, and our strong cash flow and risk management, things like that really pay off. So I don't root for a recession. I don't root for tough times. But I think choppy times are times when companies with scale like GE tend to do a little bit better."

Yes, GE's finance division would take some lumps for another year, but the overall company growth plan was in place and was working before the crisis, and Immelt expected

GE to emerge stronger when all was said and done. He had learned in business school, after all, that the best-managed companies during the harshest times just about always end up the strongest afterward. That's how GE emerged from the Great Depression of the 1930s and the recession of the 1970s, and that's how GE would emerge from whatever it was 2008 turned out to be.

Growth outside the United States with investment in GE's health-care and infrastructure businesses, while driving GE Capital back to the area the division "grew up from" in basic lending and leasing through commercial finance, would be GE's focus, the road map to success in the future. Consequently, Immelt assumed with conviction in late 2008 that Warren Buffett would not be the only investor recognizing a good deal in GE.

"We are in this for the long term," said Immelt. "That will mean more now than ever before."

CHAPTER 15

LEADERSHIP FOR THE NEW CENTURY

"The one thing you can't get until you actually have the job is understanding context and how your company fits into the world. Until you do the job, you're not aware of the true breadth of the assignment. That's something that I've learned a ton about."

—JEFF IMMELT

Transformation almost always comes at a price in business, no matter how necessary it may be for the good of a company. That's why some leaders do not dare try it. Maintaining more of the same, with a new twist here or there, is considerably easier.

That, however, is not GE. And that is not Jeff Immelt.

He planned on retooling the company for the twenty-first century from the moment Jack Welch called him that day after Thanksgiving in 2000 to tell him he would be the company's next chairman and CEO. The company had always done it that way—building over the course of one decade to robustly deliver into the next. What Immelt did not plan on, though, was the world so drastically changing over the course of his first eight years on the job, making the task much more difficult and important.

When the changes occurred, Immelt refocused on the time-tested principle that a great company must have—long-term business principles in every process and every decision. Enron had more of a short-term culture when it came to decision making. So did WorldCom. And look where it got each of those companies. By the end of the 1990s, GE was known as much or more by investors for its quarterly earnings performances than it was as a 100-year-old reliable stalwart of U.S. and global business, and Immelt knew that the corporate engine needed rebuilding.

GE's performance culture would push as hard as ever to deliver short-term results, but the early twenty-first century was proving more of a challenge than big business had experienced in decades. Besides, most people knew that industry in the next century would not, could not, resemble the way it was in the previous 100 years. Population growth mixed with limited natural resources and global climate change meant that business should not be conducted the way it was before.

Even after the turn of the new millennium, though, the environment was anything but a hot topic, and few big companies were talking about actually fixing problems and making money on it. Americans buying bigger and bigger gas-guzzling cars seemed unconcerned with energy efficiency and the like. Immelt moved ahead with GE's ecomagination initiative even though most members of the company's leadership committee disapproved, installing measurable processes to ensure profit, and it grew from its green-solutions business to reach every corner of multidimensional GE.

At the same time, Immelt invested heavily in innovation, seeking to drive organic growth from within the company while drawing upon its "deep bench" of talent. Immelt also pushed the company across the globe in an entirely different way. As one of the world's largest corporations, GE had long been global, but Immelt did more than just expand into new areas. He changed global products and services and how the company conducted its business, often identifying and joining the best local partners. And he tied each of the initiatives together under a new corporate process designed to drive growth.

The result was explosive revenue and profit growth over the span of Immelt's first seven years on the job, with GE morphing closer to the company he began to envision during his first couple of years as leader.

Nothing is ever perfect, of course. The company, according to Immelt, made a few costly decisions in its finance business during the height of the money bubble, gaining too much consumer exposure while moving away from its core strength of commercial lending. But mistakes bring valuable lessons. Before the dramatic events of late 2008 GE was already changing its lending focus to more closely match its industrial business, but efforts in the crisis were ramped up with a decided shift toward the long term. That refocus, combined with the company's already growing global products and services, had GE positioned to capitalize on the twenty-first century the same way the company had most of the century before—as an innovative stalwart.

Immelt had taken some lumps along the way in his first eight years on the job, but the day will come, wrote *Esquire* magazine in late 2008 when it named Immelt to its list of the

75 most important people in the twenty-first century, in the context of the GE chairman and CEO being viewed as the "prototypical leader for the new century."

"That day is not here yet, but it will come," *Esquire* stated.

Immelt understands that there is a typical lag time between corporate reality and Wall Street understanding in the world of big business. Investors are often slow to come back to what they have left, just as they often hang on too long to what they liked. Add in the fact, says Immelt, that multidimensional companies like GE often experience even more lag time between what they are doing and the results of that work, and there you have it.

Within the company, however, it was evident years into Immelt's leadership career at GE that the organization was responding. His leadership and processes were taking firm hold, and the company was moving ever closer to the future he imagined.

"It takes time," said Immelt. "When I got the job, I knew I wanted the company to be more innovative, more global, and more focused on the customers. But it does take a year or two or three to really put ideas into initiatives and get the team aligned. And you've got to get enough results in the pipeline so that when you talk about the things, people aren't going to say, 'You know, that's a bunch of you-know-what.' I can say, 'We're doing imagination breakthroughs, and, by the way, here are 20 examples that closed last year.' It does take time to get there."

It takes longer than he thought, perhaps, but neither Immelt nor anyone else imagined the chain of catastrophic events that would unfold during his first years on the job. Fortunately, though, he believes strongly in lessons learned from his earlier days on sports playing fields.

Immelt understands that good bounces just about always balance out the bad if you have patience. And in the end, the best team usually wins.

AFTERWORD

C alamitous effects from the early twenty-first century's great economic fall left almost no big business standing in 2009 as it was before. Frozen credit, spending retraction, and declining confidence attacked corporations with vigor, altering planning and results in both the short-term and long-term in ways the corporate world has not experienced in decades, if ever. Each passing day and week yielded mounting casualties that might previously have seemed unlikely, if not impossible.

Japanese automaker Toyota, one of the world's most studied and respected companies, steeped in culture and processes, delayed a new manufacturing plant under construction and lost money for the first time in more than 50 years. Banking conglomerate Citigroup was being split into many tiny pieces following record financial losses and evidence that sustainability was questionable. Software stalwart Microsoft fell short of earnings estimates for the final quarter of 2008 and announced its first-ever significant job layoffs in early 2009, cutting more than 5,000 positions. And global economic bellwether General Electric was eliminating jobs, restructuring divisions, and facing less-than-expected earnings and growth and a stock price that dipped to a 10-year low.

Amid the stumbles, an appearance of leveling occurred in the marketplace as the once-mighty revealed imperfections and the once-infallible showed they were still, in fact, fallible. Veracity in business, though, is often deceptive, particularly in the most difficult times when casualties become lumped together. Individual corporations' disastrous results, which seem equal in scale when examining the marketplace, have in reality varying degrees of impact based on each company's level of preparedness. Some were built to withstand heavy blows and to get back up and fight, while others were not engineered to fight at all. The great differentiator, then, becomes training and preparedness, and the ability to draw upon true, already established strengths in adversity.

For Jeff Immelt and GE, the differentiation begins with an obsession in cultivating leaders—a strategy that began with the company's earliest leadership more than 100 years ago, grew mightily under Jack Welch in the last two decades of the twentieth century, and continues to grow as the company evolves today. Effective business leaders learn quickly that nobody, not even savviest economists, can predict the future accurately.

In 2006, for instance, many experts argued convincingly that the bursting of America's housing price bubble would be relegated to regional pockets. And midway through 2008, other experts argued that the price of a barrel of oil would not fall below $100 again ever, yet months later, oil was priced below $40 a barrel.

Reliance upon educated assumption of the future is foolish.

Reliance upon well-trained people, on the other hand, is prudent.

That is why the most striking words Immelt said to me during our time together preparing this book were related to training and human resource development.

Long before Immelt became the company's leader, GE invested more heavily in its people than probably any other company on the planet. Using its leadership center in Crotonville, New York, as a beacon of continuing and higher education, the company spent, over the span of five decades, billions of dollars and years of accumulated employee time out of the office and away from daily job requirements providing developmental instruction.

Faced with taking over as GE's leader in a period of unequaled stock price valuation and expectation, Immelt could have quietly backed away from the commitment required in cost, time, and energy, gathering every possible bit of short-term momentum. Instead, he upped the commitment, extending GE's training and education ground to the company's research center in Niskayuna, New York, and giving the Jack Welch Leadership Center in Crotonville even more support through funding and programming.

As I sat in Immelt's office one September day in 2008 while the global economic meltdown was gathering significant momentum, he could have easily backed away from the commitment to building leaders. But he told me in certain terms that no matter how tough the fight became, his and the company's commitment to training its people would not only continue, but also would be enhanced.

GE, he explained, does not teach its people to be the best in wind energy, medical imaging, or jet engine design. Instead, it teaches its people how to be leaders. GE, he said, teaches its people how to perform, problem-solve, and drive change, regardless of the circumstances.

GE'S GROWTH AS A PROCESS CHART

GROWTH AS A PROCESS

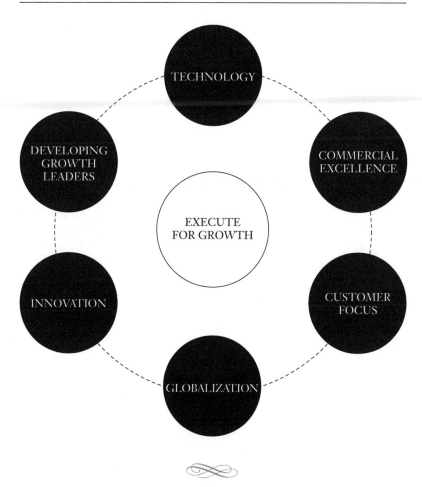

GE'S OPERATIONAL EXCELLENCE CHART

OPERATIONAL EXCELLENCE

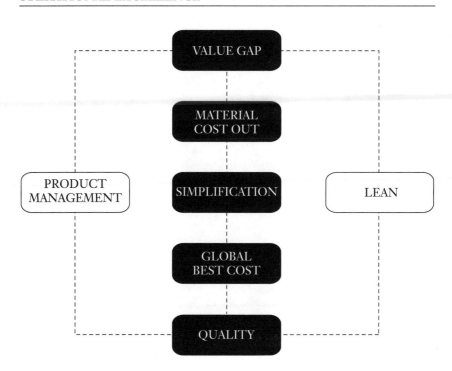

CAREER TIMELINE FOR JEFF IMMELT AT GE

1974   Immelt graduates from Cincinnati's Finneytown High School.

1978   Earns degree in applied math from Dartmouth; takes job at Procter & Gamble.

1980   Enters master's program at Harvard Business School.

1982   Begins career at GE in commercial leadership program.

1983   Becomes manager in business development for GE Plastics.

1984   Promoted to manager of Dallas district sales, GE Plastics.

1986   Elevated to general manager, western region sales, GE Plastics.

1987   Named general manager for new business development and marketing development, GE Plastics.

1987   Youngest GE manager to attend company's executive development course at Crotonville.

1989   Transfers to Louisville, Kentucky, to become president of consumer service, GE Appliances.

1990   Passes big test in successfully managing massive recall of faulty refrigerator compressors.

1991   Named vice president of worldwide marketing and product management, GE Appliances.

1992   Returns to Dallas as vice president of the commercial division for GE Plastics Americas.

1993   Promoted to division vice president and general manager, GE Plastics Americas.

1994 Overcomes pricing problem at GE Plastics, negotiating with General Motors CEO Roger Smith.

1997 Named president and CEO, GE Medical Systems.

2000 Welch tells Immelt he will be the company's next leader. Becomes president and chairman-elect, GE; elected to company board of directors.

2001 Succeeds Jack Welch as chairman and CEO, General Electric Company, becoming company's 12th leader since company founding in the 1800s.

2001 Watches events of 9/11 on company-owned television network from hotel room in Seattle just four days after taking GE's leadership job.

2002 Successfully acquires wind business from Enron.

2003 GE business NBC wins bid to broadcast 2010 and 2012 Olympic games for $2.2 billion.

2003 Merges media and entertainment company Vivendi with NBC.

2003 Buys European health solutions provider Amersham for $9.5 billion.

2004 Along with Rolls-Royce, wins engine contract for Boeing 7E7 Dreamliner; valued at $40 billion over 25 years.

2005 Launches companywide Ecomagination business initiative.

2005 Realigns GE's 11 businesses into 6 industry-focused groupings.

2006 GE identified as world leader in desalination and water reuse systems.

2007 Sells GE Plastics unit for $11.66 billion.

2007 *Fortune* magazine names GE America's most admired company.

2008 GE, Algeria opens Africa's largest seawater desalination plant; will serve up to 2 million residents.

2008 GE successfully mass produces OLEDs (organic light-emitting diodes); says OLEDs might one day replace traditional light bulb.

2008 Sells $3 billion in GE preferred stock to Berkshire Hathaway in deal with legendary investor Warren Buffett.

GE'S RESULTS UNDER JEFF IMMELT (2001–2007)*

Category	2001	2007	Net Change
Revenues	$107,558	$172,738	$65,180
Net earnings	$13,791	$22,208	$8,417
Dividends declared	$6,555	$11,713	$5,158
Total assets of continuing operations	$373,550	$788,568	$415,018
Total assets	$495,012	$795,337	$300,325
Long-term borrowings	$77,818	$319,015	$241,197
Shares outstanding (avg., in thousands)	9,932,245	10,182,083	249,838
Market capitalization (year-end share price)†	$398,084,380,600	$377,449,816,810	($20,634,562,790)
Price per share (year end)	$40.08	$37.07	($3.01)
Total employees	310,000	327,000	17,000
Net earnings per share	$1.37	$2.18	$0.81
Return on average shareowner equity	24.7%	20.4%	(4.3%)

* *Source for all results from GE annual reports. Dollar amounts are in millions except for market cap, share price, and earnings per share.*
† *Market cap has decreased because of issuance of equity and loss of share price.*

GE'S LEADERSHIP HISTORY

Charles Coffin (president, 1896–1913; chairman, 1913–1922). Guided company through depression of 1893 and his calm, timely leadership helped establish GE as a premier U.S. corporation. Initiated procedure for training and grading executives on performance measurables.

E. W. Rice (president, 1913–1922). Among the company's first executives to recognize the value of investing heavily in research, hiring the best and giving them latitude. He established the company's research center.

Gerard Swope (president, 1922–1940, 1942–1945). An engineer by trade, he brought a deep sense of patriotism and civic service to GE. He further developed GE's principle of executive training and leadership cultivation from within.

Owen Young (chairman, 1922–1939, 1942–1945). Led GE to diversify which perhaps saved the company during the Great Depression. Pushed the company's expansion into consumer appliances and associated support in marketing and financing. Centralized the organization's multiple businesses which led to a unified and contemporary company.

Charles Wilson (president, 1945–1950, 1940–1942). A statesman whose GE career spanned more than 50 years, Wilson left the company in 1942 to serve President Roosevelt as vice chairman of the war production board.

Phillip Reed (chairman, 1940–1942, 1945–1958). Leader in international public affairs who helped GE gain global awareness, education, and opportunities.

Ralph Cordiner (president, 1950–1958; chairman and CEO, 1958–1963). Credited with developing GE's postwar reorganization and decentralization program which brought new flexibility and a sharper focus to specific markets. The decentralized multidivisional corporation emerged as a model in U.S. business. Cordiner wanted the larger, diversified company to operate as a collection of small businesses. He implemented employee evaluations and the beginnings of GE's promote-from-within culture.

Gerald Phillippe (president, 1961–1963; chairman, 1963–1967). Humanitarian who founded the the Urban Coalition, Phillippe was known for applying business solutions to urban problems.

Fred Borch (president and CEO, 1963–1967; chairman and CEO 1967–1972). Known for getting the most out of employees, Borch led GE's first growth revolution, nearly doubling the size of the company in terms of sales and earnings between 1963 and 1972. He also further developed Cordiner's established human resources strategies, establishing a slating evaluation system of managers.

Reginald Jones (chairman and CEO, 1972–1981). Continued GE's growth culture, doubling sales and earnings during his decade-long tenure. Pushed for growth through more measured, strategic planning. Considered by peers as the most respected business leader in the United States, according to a leading publication.

John (Jack) Welch Jr. (chairman and CEO, 1981–2001). Increased annual revenues in two decades from just more than $26 billion to $130 billion. Cultivated managers through training and motivation, pushing them to exceed stretch limits. Instituted boundaryless communication and bottom-up employee initiatives. Named manager of the century in 1999 by a leading business publication.

Jeffrey Immelt (chairman and CEO, 2001–present). Took over company at the end of a historic bull market. Then almost immediately experience the 9/11 terrorist attacks and U.S. corporate downfall. Restructuring company for new century of business through global expansion, clean energy initiatives, and infrastructure development. Increased research and development spending while maintaining employee training. In his eight-year tenure, he has led the company to an annual increase in revenues of more than $60 billion.

NOTES

The best understanding comes from going, seeing, and learning for yourself, and I am grateful that GE allowed me to do just that for this book. Interviews with key company executives, including Jeff Immelt, John Rice, and John Little, provided deep insight as did visits to key company facilities including those in Atlanta, Georgia; Fairfield, Connecticut; and Niskayuna, New York. Throughout the book, information gathered during the firsthand interviews and trips serves along with transcripts from about half a dozen public talks given by Jeff Immelt as the backbone of information. Dozens of secondary sources were consulted as well, and credit is given when applicable. A source of particular note that should be mentioned is the video file of Jeff Immelt's November 2007 talk at Cornell University, which was provided by Cornell University's Department of Applied Economics and Management. This talk was simultaneously broadcast via satellite to five other universities. Quotes from this Immelt speech are used in several places in the manuscript, as are quotes from other public speeches made by Immelt. However, most other quotes used in the book from Immelt were obtained firsthand unless specifically noted.

Chapter 1

Page 9 **"My parents believed . . ."** Jim Citrin, May 10, 2008, yahoo.com, "Leadership by Example."

Page 10 **"Sports and other . . ."** Ibid.

Page 12 **"He was the best . . ."** *BusinessWeek*, April 29, 2002, "The Education of Jeff Immelt."

Page 16 **"My manager called and said . . ."** *Harvard Business Review*, May 1, 2007. "GE's Jeff Immelt: The Voyage from MBA to CEO."

Page 16 **"To what do you . . ."** Ibid.

Chapter 2

Page 20 **Immelt's physical transformation . . .** *Time*, September 10, 2001, "Jack Who?"

Page 20 **"It was hard . . ."** Ibid.

Page 21 **"I did not have one . . ."** Fast Company, June 2005, "The Fast Company Interview: Jeff Immelt."

Page 22 **"I'd say, 'Here's the Weibel curve . . .'"** Ibid.

Page 24 **"Jeff," Welch told Immelt . . .** Ibid

Page 25 **"Look," Immelt replied . . .** Ibid

Page 26 **"I was a thousand . . ."** *BusinessWeek*, September 6, 2001, GE's Jeff Immelt: His Own Man

Page 30 **Welch, wrote one scribe, was revered . . .** Ibid.

Page 34 **"It was just the two . . ."** *USA Today*, January 3, 2007, "Home Depot Boots CEO Nardelli."

Page 35 **"Everybody at GE . . ."** *Time*, September 10, 2001, "Jack Who?"

Chapter 3

Page 39 **"This is not just a job . . ."** *BusinessWeek*, April 29, 2002, "The Education of Jeff Immelt."

Page 41 **"Let's categorize September 11 . . ."** www.businessweek.com, January 28, 2002, "Q & A: A Talk with Jeff Immelt."

Page 46 **"The first year . . ."** www.businessweek.com, September 11, 2006, "General Electric, the Immelt Way."

Chapter 5

Page 63   **"I never had a fear . . ."** *Fast Company*, June 2005, "The Fast Company Interview: Jeff Immelt."

Page 63   **"We talked about acquisitions . . ."** *BusinessWeek*, April 29, 2002, "The Education of Jeff Immelt."

Page 64   **"The week of Gross's article . . ."** Ibid.

Page 66   **"I think it is one . . ."** *The Financial Times*, December 27, 2003, "Man of the Year."

Page 73   **"Shit, I hate it when the stock price goes down . . ."** *BusinessWeek*, April 29, 2002, "The Education of Jeff Immelt."

Page 74   **"A 65-year-old . . ."** *Nightly Business Report*, PBS, September 6, 2006.

Chapter 6

Page 77   **". . . if we can spur our growth rate ..."** *Harvard Business Review*, June 2006, "Growth as a Process."

Page 92   **"Nobody is allowed not to play . . ."** Ibid.

Page 94   **"We're now in a slow-growth . . ."** Ibid.

Page 95   **"Achieving this kind . . ."** Wisconsin Technology Network, www.wisctechnology.com, July 13, 2006

Chapter 7

Page 100   **"The cross-business fertilization . . ."** Reuters, February 7, 2007.

Page 109   **"First, 25 years ago . . ."** *Fortune*, December 11, 2006. "Q & A: On the Hot Seat."

Chapter 8

Page 112   **Try telling that . . .** *The Planet Newsletter*, Sierra Club, October 2000.

Page 115   **"They said, 'This is stupid . . .'"** *BusinessWeek*, March 4, 2008, "The Issue: Immelt's Unpopular Idea."

Page 116   **"There's about five times . . ."** Ibid.

Page 121   **"There were plenty of guys . . ."** *Harvard Business Review*, June 2006, "Growth as a Process."

Page 129   **"There has to be . . ."** *Portfolio*, September 18, 2008, "GE and Google Announce '21st- Century' Electrical System."

Chapter 9

Page 134 **"I always tell . . ."** *Fast Company*, June 2005, "The Fast Company Interview: Jeff Immelt."

Page 135 **"Core values really . . ."** *Harvard Business Review*, June 2006, "Growth as a Process."

Page 137 **"I'm less trusting . . ."** *Fast Company*, June 2005, "The Fast Company Interview: Jeff Immelt."

Page 140 **How a company instills a performance culture . . .** *McKinsey on Culture*, white paper written by Scott Keller and Carolyn Aiken, February 1, 2006.

Page 141 **The benefits of being . . .** *McKinsey on Culture*, white paper written by Scott Keller and Carolyn Aiken, February 1, 2006.

Page 145 **"We had planned . . ."** *USA Today*, April 11, 2008.

Page 146 **"We let people down . . ."** *Wall Street Journal*, April 17, 2008.

Page 146 **"I want to set the record straight . . ."** *BusinessWeek*, April 17, 2008, Jack Welch on Jeff Immelt.

Page 147 **"Constant reinvention . . ."** *Business 2.0 Magazine*, July 1, 2004, "GE Sees the Light by Learning to Manage Innovation."

Page 148 **"I was taking over . . ."** *Fortune*, December 11, 2006, "Q & A: On the Hot Seat."

Chapter 10

Page 154 **"If you run a big . . ."** *Harvard Business Review*, June 2006, "Growth as a Process."

Page 156 **"I inherited a company . . ."** *Fortune*, December 11, 2006, "Q & A: On the Hot Seat."

Page 157 **"At some moment . . ."** *Bloomberg News*, March 27, 2007.

Page 159 **"I'm an optimist . . ."** *Fast Company*, June 2005, "The Fast Company Interview: Jeff Immelt."

Page 159 **The Commercial Council also began . . .** *Harvard Business Review*, May 1, 2007, "GE's Jeff Immelt: The Voyage from MBA to CEO."

Page 162 **"If I want people . . ."** Ibid.

Page 163   **"We spent a half day . . ."** Jim Citrin, May 10, 2008, yahoo.com, "Leadership by Example."

Page 166   **"I knew if I could define a process . . ."** *Harvard Business Review*, May 1, 2007, "GE's Jeff Immelt: The Voyage from MBA to CEO."

Chapter 11

Page 168   **"'Learning,' Welch said, 'it's all about . . .'"** Robert Slater, *Jack Welch & the GE Way*, McGraw-Hill, 1998.

Page 169   **"The philosophy is . . ."** Ibid.

Page 170   **"Every time we sit down . . ."** Jim Citrin, May 10, 2008, yahoo.com, "Leadership by Example."

Page 172   **"To get a lot out of benchmarking . . ."** Ibid.

Page 175   **"I benefit from the chance . . ."** Ibid.

Chapter 12

Page 178   **"A key GE strength . . ."** *Harvard Business Review*, May 1, 2007, "GE's Jeff Immelt: The Voyage from MBA to CEO."

Page 179   **"In China, the government is the customer . . ."** *Manufacturing & Technology News*, November 30, 2007.

Page 185   **"Everyone tells me about the disadvantages of conglomerates . . ."** *Jack Welch and the GE Way.*

Page 189   **"Our businesses are closely . . ."** *General Electric Annual Report*, 2004.

Chapter 13

Page 196   **" . . . our culture is based . . ."** *New York Times*, October 5, 2007.

Page 200   **"Sure, we could keep buying . . ."** Ibid.

Page 203   **"You move more outside . . ."** *USA Today*, July 22, 2008.

Page 206   **"This segment contains many of the fastest-growing . . ."** Ibid.

Chapter 14

Page 212   **"We ought to be trading . . ."** *The New York Times*, March 14, 2008.

Page 215   **"We do boring stuff . . ."** Reuters, September 17, 2008.

Page 223   **"Certainly nothing had happened . . ."** Reuters, October 9, 2008.

Page 226   **"In the last three or four years . . ."** *Nightly Business Report*, PBS, February 6, 2008.

Chapter 15

Page 232   **"It takes time . . ."** *Fast Company*, June 2005, "The Fast Company Interview: Jeff Immelt."

ACKNOWLEDGMENTS

Thanks to friend and researcher Tim Threadgill, who provided invaluable help on this project. He looked deeply into GE along with me, compiling data and pointing out key elements of Jeff Immelt's and GE's strategy and results. For his services, I am grateful.

Appreciation is also given to my McGraw-Hill editor, Knox Huston. Having worked with Knox on my first book when he worked for a different publisher, I knew the moment we talked about this project that he was the editor I wanted to work with. Each step along the way proved that my initial instinct was right. He wanted a book that showed depth of both leader and organization, and he provided editorial leeway and guidance in my attempt to deliver. His knowledge of GE from previous books and management study in general was helpful, and his insight into what makes a business book successful was invaluable. Huston is everything an author wants and more, making this project immensely enjoyable.

Others at McGraw-Hill deserving particular mention include McGraw-Hill business publisher Herb Schaffner; Keith Pfeffer, senior director of national accounts; Mary Glenn, editorial director; marketing manager Gaya Vinay; key account sales representatives Eileen Lamadore and Richard Callison; and publicist Ann Pryor.

At GE, thank you to Jeffrey DeMarrais, who arranged executive interviews, provided corporate insight, and answered my many questions. Appreciation also goes to Gary Sheffer, GE's chief corporate spokesman, who helped provide access and never asked for anything in return. GE is a big but responsive company, which is all a writer can ask for.

Finally, thank you to The Seaside Institute in Seaside, Florida, for a month-long residency and the opportunity to escape to create.

INDEX

ABOUT THE AUTHOR

D avid Magee is the author of *How Toyota Became #1*; *Turaround: How Carlos Ghosn Rescued Nissan*; *The John Deere Way*; and *Ford Tough*. His books have been reviewed in *The Wall Street Journal*, *The Harvard Business Review*, and *Newsweek*. His Web site is www.david-magee.com.